68

© 2022 McSweeney's Quarterly Concern and the contributors, San Francisco, California. ASSISTED BY: Annie Dills, Francesca Hodges, Lucy Huber, Lizzy Lemieux, Conor O'Brien, Raj Tawney, Selena Trager, Alvaro Villanueva. COPY EDITOR: Caitlin Van Dusen. DIRECTOR OF SALES AND DISTRIBUTION: Dan Weiss. OPERATIONS MANAGER: Eric Cromie. TECHNOLOGY DIRECTOR: Nikky Southerland. ART DIRECTOR: Sunra Thompson. FOUNDING EDITOR: Dave Eggers. PUBLISHER & EXECUTIVE DIRECTOR: Amanda Uhle. EXECUTIVE EDITOR: Claire Boyle. VISITING EDITOR: Daniel Gumbiner.

COVER ART: Daniele Castellano.

INTERIOR ILLUSTRATIONS: Wesley Allsbrook.

MCSWEENEY'S LITERARY ARTS FUND BOARD OF DIRECTORS: Natasha Boas, Carol Davis, Brian Dice (president), Isabel Duffy-Pinner, Caterina Fake, Hilary Kivitz, Jordan Kurland, Nion McEvoy, Gina Pell, Jeremy Radcliffe, Jed Repko, Vendela Vida.

Printed in Canada.

DEAR MCSWEENEY'S,
This past April marked the twentieth anniversary of *Bend It Like Beckham*, easily one of the most iconic films to grace our collective theaters and television screens (or maybe just mine?) during the 2000s. I've been trying not to rewatch too many of my trash favorites recently, because I'm pretending that's the reason I haven't been more productive or written better poems, but because it's been twenty years, and *Bend It* is finally available on HBO Max, I made an exception.

The movie really has everything one needs from art: nostalgia, queer potential spelled out only in subtext, cinematography so low-quality it could have been filmed on a flip phone, mother issues, a subtle interaction between postcolonialism and neoliberalism, and, of course, football shootball. As someone who has been labeled "a simp for earnestness" by an ex, I also mostly find the cast deeply endearing (except the dude who plays Jess's dad, because he is 100 percent an extremist right-wing politician now). They were handed some, at times, borderline appalling dialogue, but, by god, did they give it their all.

In one of the pivotal scenes, the protagonist, Jess, is trying to convince her parents to let her play football yet again. "Anyone can cook aloo gobi," she says, "but who can bend a ball like Beckham?" What a defining moment that was for twelve-year-old me: fighting against all odds (or so it seemed) to make it onto the under-seventeen basketball team and generally just failing spectacularly at gender the entire time.

As an adult, I find, I've grown more indifferent to the art of football or of any sport, really, and have definitely learned to better appreciate a good aloo gobi. For the last two years, I—like everyone I know—have been cooking more than I used to. I'm an anxious cook, but I do like to feed folks I love, and aloo gobi is one of the four dishes I can cook adequately enough to feed them.

The trick is to sprinkle the cauliflower and potatoes with salt, pepper, turmeric, and oil, and roast them separately. This way, while they're in the oven, I can make the masala on the stovetop and then toss everything together at the end. The first time I did this, I was so proud of myself. I tried to tell my mom what a difference roasting makes instead of turning everything into a boiled mush on the stove and she indignantly responded, "You cook like someone who has no children to look after." I think she was just upset that I had insinuated that her aloo gobi was a boiled mush (which was not my intention), and while what she said is technically and literally true, I was still offended. Even though I've been progressively working on not getting offended by things my mother says.

That's an easier task when you're separated by two continents. Or it used to be. I'm sorry; I've been trying not to let diasporic angst upset everything I write lately, but it's hard. In September 2020, with nothing to do but worry about their lives and miss their children, my parents mastered the art of googling and somehow found a podcast episode on which I'd appeared to discuss queerness in fan fiction.

*Bend It Like Beckham* was, in several ways, my queer awakening. It solved, or rather confused, a lot of questions I had about my preteen self. Was Parminder Nagra's character in love with Jules, or was I in love with Jess? Why was the montage of Keira Knightley hitting a soccer ball with her head keeping me up every night? Was I attracted to Jonathan Rhys Meyers in a cricket sweater? Did I want to be Jonathan Rhys Meyers in a cricket sweater? Did I want to be the cricket sweater hugging Jonathan Rhys Meyers?

That's how my mother found out her child was undeniably gay—through a podcast audio clip of them describing (on repeat) their thoughts about seeing Jonathan Rhys Meyers in a white vest, and their longing for Jess and Jules and what could have been.

The one consistent thread in the movie is this: Jess always gets caught. She gets caught when she lies about a fake job and goes to train with her teammates instead. She gets caught when she uses her sister's wedding funds to buy soccer boots and when she pretends to be sick so she can slip out to play a match. It's only when her father truly accepts her "identity" as a footballer that she plays and wins the match, and her freedom.

Luckily, another thing that's easier when you're separated by two continents is living a life your family doesn't know about. I'm neither fresh out of high school nor sneaking out to play football, but, at twenty-eight years old, I have hidden three relationships and two cross-country moves from my mother. Each time I've taken a trip back to

New York this year, I've prayed harder than ever for nothing to go wrong: for each flight to be safe, for each cab ride not to end in an accident. Not because I'm worried about my life, but because I don't want my mother to find out that her adult child is somewhere other than where they're expected to be.

I'm not too sure of what I'm trying to say here, but I do want to point out that my mother, like any self-respecting deshi, also loves *Bend It Like Beckham*. And she loves me even when we unknowingly play out the exact same conversations that Jess and Mrs. Bhamra have. And I love her, even though, to be completely honest, her aloo gobi remains superior. And we've done what we do best, which is to forget that the queer podcast ever happened, so we can love each other the way (sometimes the only way) we have learned to: by knowing as little about each of our individual lives as is necessary. So here's to celebrating twenty years of *Bend It Like Beckham*, here's to teenage me gaping and drooling at the Hounslow Harriers, who will all, God willing, play for England one day, and here's to my mother, who sat through at least twenty-three rewatches with me without suspecting a thing. It's like Keira Knightley says when Jules's mom asks her if she's dating Jess: "Anyway, being a lesbian's not that big a deal."

SRESHTHA SEN
LAS VEGAS, NV


DEAR MCSWEENEY'S,
I recently purchased the Kanye West/ Yeezy Gap Round Jacket. The one that

people a decade younger than me covet enough to set alarms on their phones for the wee hours of the morning on the off chance that they might be able to part with their money to acquire it.

You know the one, surely. The blue puffer jacket that looks like a car airbag deployed on you from your closet. It's massive, awkward, and shockingly impractical for a person who lives in sunny Los Angeles. On this front, I can relate. I often feel just like this bulbous piece of two-hundred-dollar outerwear—bulging at the seams, with no sense of purpose whatsoever. Did I mention this jacket has no buttons and no zippers?

I have worn the Yeezy Round Jacket a grand total of two times. Once was to photograph myself for the purposes of getting engagement on social media. "Hey, look! I bought the thing that makes me resemble that poor girl who turned into a grape in *Willy Wonka and the Chocolate Factory*." Anytime you can procure something coveted, rare, or outré, you simply must share it with the world. The reaction to the Instagram post was vigorous: "Wow." "Cool." "What made you do this?" "Aren't you almost 40?"

The second time I wore the jacket was to get coffee, which is one of the rare times I leave the house without my four-year-old in tow. Believe me when I say that the garment was not designed for automobile travel. This jacket is voluminous. It takes up space. It asserts itself. I had a hard time reaching the buttons on my driver's-side console because of the sheer amount of nylon bulging out from my body.

*Where's the ignition? Is that the right button to roll my window down or is that for the passenger side? Which gear am I in?* As I mentioned, it looked like I was wearing an airbag, which meant passersby might have thought I'd recently emerged from a catastrophic fender bender. Perhaps the jacket does have a practical purpose: preventing severe injury in the event of a collision.

When I finally reached the coffee shop, I could feel the eyes on me. Of course, eyes can't speak or declare their intentions. Eyes are instruments of inquisition, but the nature of their judgment is uncertain. Were the people in line with me in awe of my purchase? Were they delighted to finally see one of these jackets out in the wild? Or were they horrified by how brazenly I flaunted this bizarre fashion choice? I'd like to think I inspired them to tell their friends what they had witnessed, to ponder their own place in the sartorial landscape, and to maybe consider a jacket that's way too large to wear in public. But I'll never know.

The thing you're thinking about right now is probably: Why? Why would I buy a jacket that I don't even seem to enjoy wearing? The simple truth is that I bought it to sell it. There are thousands of people out there who will pay more than what I paid to own the Yeezy Round Jacket. Objects that have no value to one person could have great meaning for someone else. There are numerous clichés about this particular phenomenon that you probably are familiar with, but I refuse to use them, because this is a classy literary magazine.

This is a truism I wish I had applied earlier to my own life. I dated a lot when I was younger. Like, a lot. I am, sadly, addicted to gaining approval from women. Place the blame on my emotionally withholding parents, the proliferation of heteronormative romantic narratives in mass media, or plain loneliness in the face of a technological dystopia that devalues any of our contributions to society that don't involve consuming gleaming, pocket-size trinkets that can tell you the weather. Whatever the reason, I have always needed everyone to love me equally, with a level of fervor that would be rightly labeled unhealthy by any functioning clinical professional. I think that's called narcissism.

Unfortunately, I am not equally desirable to all people. I've had to learn that there are varying degrees of "like" in life. I am, like my giant blue jacket, unlovable to some. I have been traded in for a slightly newer model before. I might be again. I'm massive, awkward, and shockingly impractical. But maybe that's part of my charm.

DAVE SCHILLING
LOS ANGELES, CA

DEAR MCSWEENEY'S,
Listen. We don't have much time. What do you want to accomplish before you die? I use the word *accomplish* here in the broadest sense. For instance, "existing in the present moment" would be a significant goal. I've recently worked my way into an idea for a film titled "The Unified Theory of David Lynch." It relies on the premise that David Lynch is possibly from outer space or else has access to the wisdom of outer space. When I suggested to a friend that "alien" was perhaps the best explanation I had ever heard for David Lynch, he responded: "I am not ruling it out for even a second." A particular strength of mind possessed by this friend is that he *never* rules out aliens, goblins, bog monsters, et cetera. He is mentally prepared for anything.

Next considered: Is David Lynch either an alien who landed on Earth or descended from aliens who landed on Earth many generations ago, *or* did he connect with alien intelligence via transcendental meditation, "giving [him] cosmic knowledge which made him this way," as my friend put it? We both concurred that the TM angle made the most sense—*sense* in this case referring to how this option opened up opportunities to make meaning rather than limiting them.

Then a second, less serious friend texted the following:

Remember when he rescued the five Woody Woodpecker dolls from a roadside stand and hung out with them for years, but then their energy turned dark on him and so "they're not in [his] life anymore?"

I did not remember this. But it seemed yet another plot point in a movie that was writing itself.

So we had a plausible situation: David Lynch connecting with aliens via TM, and "what looks like garbled behavior to us is just a by-product of traveling between realms" (as my friend put it)—but still I harbored concerns. You see, I didn't want David Lynch to think that I was making fun of him, that I thought this was some sort of joke, because I wasn't, and I don't. I think there is a funniness to the idea in the way that there is humor in *Twin Peaks*; that is, the humor exists, but we are interested in it not so much as humor but as a discrete yet essential part of the cosmology of the story, a manifestation of consciousness in a work of art that serves as a blueprint of its creator. We are interested in Lynch's humor insomuch as it is a view into Lynch's brain and not for its comic relief, because there is no relief that comes with his humor. It is serious humor. If there is one thing David Lynch isn't interested in, it's relief.

And so I envision "The Unified Theory of David Lynch" to be funny, but in a serious way, as it undertakes an earnest investigation of the spiritual and stellar origins and emanations of David Lynch. As I wrote in my diary on March 18, 2022: "The movie itself becomes a thing Lynch has willed into being and becomes part of the argument for its own existence." Ideally, David Lynch would also direct and act in this film, if he isn't infuriated and/or offended by the idea of it.

Look. I am the first to admit I don't have it all figured out. I am the first to admit I know less the further I go. A few months ago, my seven-year-old son was tasked by his second-grade teacher with interviewing the oldest person in his family, which turned out to be my father, aged eighty-three, who is himself a Lynchian sort of character, or

at least he is within my own psychological drama.

The last question my son posed to my father was this: "How would you like to be remembered?"

And my father said to him: "I want everyone to know I wasn't pretending."

Who could have fathomed such an answer? And who could ever live up to it?

I have a sense that stories do not stretch across time but instead impale themselves through generations, proceed from director to dream, from screen to viewer, and descend infinitely downward through layers of meaning. You can go as far as you are willing to take it. Don't rule out anything. You can and you will TM yourself all the way to the aliens. Stories are not a joke. They are serious. They are our salvation. David Lynch would agree.

Sincerely,

RACHEL YODER
IOWA CITY, IA


DEAR MCSWEENEY'S,

Have you ever had this experience: you're looking forward to a normal day, sipping coffee, hitting up the family thread with a "morning!" text while scrolling through some journalism, and then, boom—you discover that the recycling system in the United States is completely broken? Well, maybe you've heard this a couple times over the years, but now you've crossed an arbitrary threshold of understanding and you can't go back? Like now you absolutely know that most of our recycling isn't actually being recycled? Sucks, huh? But years later, you're still checking plastic takeout containers for that triangular recycling symbol like it means something? Like some desperate chump?

I can't be the only one who refuses to stop recycling, right? Though of course, I'm wondering, Why do I still do this in the face of blatant facts? Would I be one of those people that keeps showing up to the office even during an apocalypse? Even though I don't have an office job? Should I apply to an office job so I can have a routine to cling to in case of emergency? Am I in denial? Is it still denial if I'm admitting it? Am I so desperate to feel like a good person that I would live a lie? If I had a virtuous office job, would my need to recycle disappear? Do those kinds of office jobs exist?

Or is it not about pretending to be good, it's about practicing being good, and practicing is worthwhile because we should be ready for the moment our recycling system works? If that were true, wouldn't it be cynical to quit now? Or is recycling nothing more than a thoughtless habit honed through my upbringing? When I was a child, my mom found paper that I had thoughtlessly thrown into the trash and she looked at me all betrayed and said: "I never thought I'd have a kid who would do something like that," and that must've fucked me up, right? But it's been multiple decades since then, and isn't it possible for a habit to begin as an empty ritual and evolve into something meaningful? I mean, isn't everything like that, rote memorization before meaning, like knowing the

lyrics to "Too Close" by Next before understanding them? Which is crazy because that song is extremely literal?

What's wrong with believing in recycling, anyway? Isn't believing in recycling the same thing as believing that nothing is truly permanent? That everything comes back to haunt us anyway, so what if we made that into a positive, functional thing? Are you thinking, Samantha, if you choose belief over facts, then you won't be moved to be part of the solution? And what if I responded that I wasn't going to be part of the solution either way— and if you knew me you would know that, and you clearly don't, because you called me "Samantha" and nobody does that, not even my mother?

Can't you understand why I would need this belief system? That my utter lack of spirituality is one of my biggest shortcomings? Do you know how alienating that can be for someone who grew up in Berkeley, California? Could you ever understand what it's like to be from the Bay and only do yoga for the exercise? To spend hours of your life sitting through Rumi quotes while you plan your exit from the studio? Have you kept your eyes open during the final meditation, against the teacher's wishes, because you're desperate to make eye contact with one other person who's also only there for the exercise?

Maybe what I don't understand is anything at all? Is that what I'm scared of? Admitting that many genres of music and abstract visual art have no effect on me whatsoever and yet, I'm not exactly logical either? I wonder if modern art is a worthwhile medium, if it's all meaningless or if I'm petty, and jealous that I've never received the level of attention people are willing to give a frame-to-frame painting of nothing but off-white? And if people do in fact appreciate visual art, at least the stuff in museums, why would their appreciation always look the same? You know what I mean? Isn't it always: staring, pointing, and selfies? At the Smithsonian's National Portrait Gallery, I saw a child run her hands over all the paintings until a security guard was like, "Um, no?" But shouldn't that be okay sometimes? Don't you find yourself wanting to touch paintings for tactile reasons? Or maybe our natural instincts are repressed because museums and galleries have rules intended to preserve the art? But even if that was true, aren't there enough true eccentrics in the world that those rules should be broken more often? Like, does it make sense that I've seen someone at the public library laughing their ass off at one of those reference atlases, and yet I've never seen anyone try and lick *The Starry Night* at MoMA, not even on Free Fridays?

So here's one theory: Maybe nothing makes sense to me except recycling? Maybe it's everything: a belief system and a spiritual practice and a tactile experience and the only form of abstraction I can get behind?

Do you ever think that one of the most satisfying and frustrating things about following a thread of questions is that it doesn't do anything to change your behavior at all, but maybe behavior's only one part of the whole life thing, anyway, right? Or am I invoking lofty, general concepts like "life" in order to get out of any further responsibility? I'm thinking… yes.

Okay, I figured it out. Thanks, McSweeney's—you were a great help!

SAM RILEY
LOS ANGELES, CA

DEAR MCSWEENEY'S,
It's finally happening, isn't it? I'm talking, of course, about the total collapse of book etiquette. Surely you've noticed the signs, the latest of which manifested on April 9, 2022, when food critic Ruth Reichl posted an Instagram video showing how she returned home from traveling to discover that her housesitting "artist friend" had reorganized *all* her books by color. A whole home library made to look like a wall at the Gap.

That's horrifying enough, but Ruth's comment makes things even worse: "We can't find anything but it looks amazing!" The first half of her remark is correct: color-coordinating books—in addition to being to interior design what the word *adulting* is to the English language—is an anti-organization method that makes finding books impossible (hence why doing it to a writer's books is deranged). It's the latter half that frightens me, with its pure feigned excitement. I must assume either that the "artist friend" was still there in the house and had forced Ruth to make the post as a final act of perversion (can we get someone to check on Ruth, actually?), or that Ruth felt social pressure to pretend she likes a color wall. (It's not possible that she actually likes it.) Thankfully, other writers expressed proper disgust, like Bill Buford, who commented, "How… upsetting!!!" Yet the fact remains that an "artist" thought this act of book aggression was okay, and then the victim had to pretend to agree. So long, sanity!

I shouldn't be surprised. Strange book energies have been afoot for years. I first knew something was off when I started getting shamed at dinner parties for mentioning that I don't lend out my books. People would scoff and press a hand to their chest and exclaim, in something like a fake British accent, "What do you *mean* you don't lend out your books? You must! Everyone lends." Who TF believes this? I call bull. I protest. And I don't lend out my books. You know who else doesn't lend out books? Bookstores. Maybe that's why they're my favorite places.

Why don't I lend? Because I cherish my books. I don't just read them; I also *re-read* them. And I use them when I'm writing other books. And other times I just stare at them or run my fingers along their spines or take long narcotized sniffs of their half-decayed bouquet—all things I wouldn't be able to do if I lent them out, because I know that once they're gone, they're gone.

This is a truth no one wants to admit, the most fundamental crack in book etiquette: people don't return books. Unsurprisingly, the worst perpetrators are the most vocal pro-lenders. Go to their homes and you'll find a five-finger library. What must that be like, moving through the world like

it's one big Sanibel beach rental where every paperback is up for grabs? How did this group impose its will on the rest of us? This is how you get to poor Ruth pretending to be excited that someone fucked with her stash.

The word *impose* makes me think of another crack. I'll admit that currently there are three books in my home that don't belong to me. But to those readers whom I can hear screaming, *Gotcha!* while sharpening their pitchforks, might I suggest that before you come to spear my guts, you first stop by your friend's and return that copy of *Braiding Sweetgrass* you borrowed on Memorial Day 2019 while "gone off the rosé," and then chew on this: I didn't borrow these books. No, it was worse. These books were *thrust* upon me.

Book thrusting: another crime of etiquette. Nowadays you can't go to anyone's house without them *demanding* you take home some text. You plead, "No, thanks, really. I've already got a pile by the bed," or "All my reading is research-driven, so this will only add clutter," but they just cackle and lick their fangs and *thrust* the book upon you anyway.

A case study: Two Halloweens ago I mentioned to my neighbor that I wanted to read William Finnegan's *Barbarian Days*. Moments later he was thrusting his copy upon me. I insisted that I needed to buy my own copy to read and mark up at my leisure, but he didn't listen. Instead he just stomped his goat hooves and shoved me and the book out the door and back home, where the book remains today. I'm looking at it now, an interloper relegated to a stack on the floor. Yet not five feet from it, mind you, is another copy of *BD* sitting smartly in the bookcase. That's *my* copy, which I bought eight months later, when I was finally ready to read *BD.* You're thinking: Why didn't you give his back before you bought your own? Because to do so would've been to admit that I hadn't read the book because I refused to read *his* copy, and because this was impossible to do, I ended up sitting on it for eight months, even though I had known on day one that I was never going to read it and could've just returned it, except, of course, that I couldn't, because any return would've required the aforementioned admission.

Now it's been two years and I've still got his copy of *BD.* I can't give it back, don't want to read it, have no need for it, can't resell it, and can't give it away. Certainly this a metaphor for something. STDs maybe? The important point is that none of this would have happened if everyone understood that your books are your books, that others' books are their books, that no one wants to be made to read anything, and that a person's reading life is one of the few private pleasures left in the world. Also, WTF do I do with this copy of *Barbarian Days?*

Wake me when it's over,

WILLIAM BREWER
OAKLAND, CA


DEAR MCSWEENEY'S,
In the last year I have read a number of essays (three) from older millennials who claim they have lost their ambition. They cite a variety of conditions, from the relentlessness of trying to make rent in the gig economy to the never-ending layoffs in dying industries to the daily burnout of parenting during a pandemic. As a former teenage overachiever turned thirty-something slacker, I should find these essays relevant. But I've gone in the opposite direction. When I was seventeen, my greatest ambition was to work at a cool magazine. Now, at thirty-two, I want to save the world.

In early 2021, I quit my gig running the social media presence for the cool magazine of my teenage dreams to take a position in the communications department of a national nonprofit focused on sustainable city building. I felt relieved at the opportunity to spend my days fighting the climate crisis. Also, the job came with benefits, and I really needed to go to the dentist. This would be my first time working in an office environment, albeit remotely. Previously, the only "real" jobs I'd had were in food service or retail (these were necessary to supplement my freelance writing work). I felt adult, nobly bowing out of the scrum of online media to work on something bigger than myself.

When I tell you how much I grew to hate this job, I need to emphasize that the fault didn't lie with any of my individual coworkers. There were plenty of smart, passionate people that I worked alongside. We answered to our supervisors, who answered to the managers, who answered to department heads, who answered to the CEO, who answered to our funders, which included a major bank that Greenpeace once ran a major campaign against, after they (the bank, not Greenpeace) funded a pipeline. Eighty percent of my days were spent in Zoom meetings during which, after endless icebreakers meant to encourage morale ("Everyone list your intention for the week along with your favorite ice cream flavor"), we would provide status updates on our respective projects, which often consisted of listing all the other meetings we were attending. Often I would play chess on my phone during these meetings, until my supervisor pulled me aside (virtually) to tell me that the managers had noticed that I was clearly distracted. I told her I was taking notes on my phone, which was obviously a lie, because why would I need to take notes during the icebreaker? It was a lie I told with conviction, like I really believed I was preserving the company's bottom line by keeping a record of the fact that Susan's favorite ice cream flavor was mint chocolate chip.

The 20 percent of the time that I wasn't in meetings, I was writing proposals or reports, pulling numbers together to justify why we were entitled to hundreds of thousands of dollars in funding. It was while writing one of these reports that I realized I was part of the problem. Instead of saving the world, I was playing online chess and letting everyone know that I preferred Ben & Jerry's nondairy Half Baked. And in doing so, I was pulling a salary out of funding earmarked for our ambiguously worded mission

statement. I made sure I had enough money in my savings account and visited the dentist, and then, at the eight-month mark, I quit.

I'm back to freelance writing (hello!), although now I spend the bulk of my days at the library, reading books on how city building policies can combat climate change. (Do you know about mandatory parking minimums? They're terrible.) I take notes on everything I'm learning in a stack of candy-colored Hilroy notebooks. I call this process "Broke Grad School." I'm not sure what my end game is, but I am learning a lot about public policy that I'm sure will come in handy when my savings run out and I try to save the world again.

I have a book coming out this year. It's called *Good Girl*, and if it sounds like I'm trying to slip a plug into this letter, I'll have you know that the book is currently slated for release only in Canada, and this is an American publication, so I'm clean. It's a novel, but several people have already asked me if it's a memoir. The heroine, Lucy, shares many biographical details with me, but that's only because my ninth-grade English teacher told me to write what I know. Lucy is constantly in a low-grade state of panic over how broken the world is. She tries, and fails, again and again, to make it better. Eventually, she learns some version of a lesson, and experiences some version of a resolution, and then the book is over. I'm already at work on a sequel.

ANNA FITZPATRICK
TORONTO, ONTARIO

# ON SOCCER SADNESS

*by* ALEJANDRO ZAMBRA

*translated by Megan McDowell*

### I.

IT WAS FOR US, when we were kids, the only kind of sadness we could perceive in our fathers' faces. We lived in a shitty world, but the only thing that really seemed to affect them was an adverse outcome in Sunday's game. Just as the two or three hours after a win were opportune for asking for permission or money, anytime our fathers sank into soccer sadness, we all knew it was better to let them deal with the defeat on their own. Pouty and wounded, they turned even more distant on those nights. They did weird things like gaze out the window at the empty street with a look of stern impotence, or listen to John Denver or Los Hermanos Zabaleta while shining their shoes frenetically, interminably. But there's no point judging them now. It's too easy. Besides, that gruff romanticism, that theoretically masculine sentimentalism, lives on in us. It's a fact that we still experience soccer sadness; the form has changed, but the feeling is alive, maybe more so than ever.

II.

There was a time, long ago, when I didn't like soccer. It wasn't that I got bored at the stadium, but I had a hard time understanding the spectacle—I proudly waved my flag and sported my Colo-Colo cap and all that, but as soon as the game started, I was more interested in pretty much anything other than what was happening on the field: the subs doing their vigorous warm-ups, for example, or the referees' timid little dance steps, or Severino Vasconcelos's dashing hair blowing in the wind. Or the heroic acrobatics of the coffee sellers, who circulated deftly through the crowd with giant thermoses hung around their necks. It was hard for me to grasp the correlation between our intense and messy pickup games and the monotonous sport I witnessed at the stadium, especially because of the almost absolute lack of goals. I have the impression that in those days I went to many games that ended nil-nil.

Going to the soccer stadium with a small child was probably a terrible idea on our fathers' part. To watch the game in relative peace, they had no choice but to ply us with ice cream, Coca-Cola, and candied peanuts. Taking us to the stadium was a mistake, but also a wager, a short- or medium-term investment, because our fathers knew that at some point we would get distracted from our distractions, and ultimately, we would be captivated by that endearing soccer slowness. In my case this happened quickly: at eight years old I was already a full-on, incorrigible fan.

A Colo-Colo fan, just like my dad. It would have been great if I had liked the rival team, or any other team at all. I can't think of a better way to kill the father—a much more gradual and effective method than the predictable grunge rebellion or the lacerating political arguments that came later. I knew of some cases of dissident kids: somehow, mysteriously, citing reasons that were unserious and banal—like that the Universidad Católica team had a nicer uniform—they managed to twist the plot, and their thwarted and perplexed fathers had no choice but to coexist with the enemy on a daily basis. And then there were those very strange cases of boys who didn't like soccer at all. I admired those boys. I didn't understand them, but I admired them.

It's not at all clear that we chose our soccer teams for ourselves. For many of us, that part of our paternal inheritance was the only one we never questioned. Really, our fathers didn't just want us to like soccer; they wanted us to like it in the specific way they did. And we loved them, of course we did. And for a time we also loved being like them. And, years later, even when we were on terrible terms with our fathers, the possibility of sublimating our problems and watching a game together granted us a reasonable amount of familial hope, a momentary truce that allowed us to maintain at least the illusion of belonging.

### III.

My relationship with soccer is not literary, but my link to literature does have, in a way, a football-istic origin. My greatest influence as a writer was not Marcel Proust's colossal novel, nor the magisterial poems of César Vallejo or Emily Dickinson or Enrique Lihn, but rather the radio transmissions of Vladimiro Mimica, the commentator for Radio Minería. No written text was as decisive for me as the elegant spoken prose of the famous "goal-singer." I even used to record the games and lie in bed to listen to the tapes, enjoying them in a purely musical sense. Thanks to his amiable mediation, even the most tedious or anodyne games seemed like memorable epic battles.

Vladimiro's voice was synonymous with the joy of soccer, but also, more than once, when I went back and listened to his play-by-plays of painful games, I'd get caught up in the magical thinking that maybe the recording would not repeat reality. Maybe, I thought, it would create a new one, a world that was not necessarily transcendent or even all that different, one that was perhaps every bit as atrocious as the real world, but where at least my team had won. Clearly, I was already suffering from a chronic case of soccer sadness.

At home and, of course, at school, I was forbidden to curse, but at the stadium I enjoyed the freedom to express myself with loud and clear profanity. There was a time when I would spend the whole game insulting the opponents and the arbitral trio. But that was only a brief period. Since we often went to doubleheaders, I would announce the preliminary game at the top of my lungs. During the week, sitting in the back row of the classroom, I would study the Chilean league programs and try to memorize the lineups of all the teams, so I usually didn't make mistakes; except for one or two isolated incidents, no one seemed to mind my performance. My job at that nonexistent radio station ended, though, when Colo-Colo came out onto the field to play the main match. Then I turned into just another fan, apprehensive and testy, watching the game with clenched teeth.

### IV.

Specialists agree that the degree of soccer sadness someone experiences is inversely proportional to their expectations of a game. Perhaps this sounds obvious. Okay, it *is* obvious, and it also seems like a theory that could apply to more than soccer, but I guess a little embellishment never hurt anyone.

In the case of those of us who are fans of the so-called big teams, expectations are always too high. We demand that our team tear it up and thump the rival week after week, so even a narrow victory in a badly played game can provoke a certain amount of soccer sadness.

That inherited triumphalism is grating: we're like those parents who, instead of congratulating and fawning over their children when they get a good grade, tell them only that they have done their duty. The situation of a fan, of a fanatic, becomes stifling; that's why we so enjoy games when we don't even slightly identify with either team playing. A kind of Zen nostalgia allows us, for once, to really appreciate the game, and to take a break from ourselves.

Maybe anticipating the hipster aesthetic, many of us have at some point fantasized about changing teams and sparing ourselves the mainstream need to win all the time, in order to savor the partial, arguable wins of a small team: staying in the first division; taking points away from the big teams and ruining their party; losing, but with dignity, after leaving it all on the field; or else enduring decisive and humiliating losses, but only after dishing out a potpourri of brutal tongue-lashings about the much-better-paid stars of the opposing team. And there are those who took that step voluntarily, but for most of us it remained no more than a shameful flight of fancy, almost always impossible to admit. Once you get to a certain age—in my case, eight years old—changing teams is simply impossible.

V.

There was no need to switch to a smaller team, really: the Chilean national selection *was* our small team. Before Marcelo Bielsa and the golden generation spoiled us and allowed us to dream of a splendid future full of World Cup wins, the Chilean selection had almost always been the team that was destined to fail, but that still, every once in a while, allowed us to flirt with glory, from a sometimes decorous and almost always enormous distance. "The Chilean team plays great / but they just can't catch a break," Nicanor Parra wrote somewhere, and that was almost always how we felt. In any case, when Chile played, our broken and divided country seemed momentarily reconciled. In fact, we did suspend our differences; we enjoyed soccer collectively, though really, more than enjoyment, it was about acknowledging a common suffering. For my generation, that suffering included the trauma of Cóndor Rojas and the deplorable incident when he faked an injury at the Maracanã Stadium. FIFA quickly discovered the trick, and they punished Rojas by banning him from play for life, and Chile by eliminating them from the qualifiers for the next World Cup. The concept of soccer sadness does not go far enough to describe what we felt in those years.

The small-team woes of the Chilean club were prodigiously offset by Colo-Colo's big-team win at the 1991 Libertadores Cup. But when our thoughts returned to our small, blackballed national team, the depression returned. We dealt with our World Cup ostracism by celebrating the individual triumphs of the few Chilean footballers who played for important teams in Europe. There was a perversion there—suddenly, for us, soccer was no longer a team sport: all we cared about was that Iván Zamorano or Marcelo Salas played for ninety minutes and scored goals. If they weren't on the pitch, we couldn't have cared less about the fate of Real Madrid or Lazio or Juventus, and we watched their games only to wish bad luck on the players who had usurped our compatriots.

VI.

I interrupt this essay to come clean about a shameful period, one that invalidates me as a fan and perhaps also as a person: for almost two years, I pretended not to like soccer.

My only excuse, legitimate but poor, is youth. Love can't serve as a mitigating circumstance, though it all started one day in the midst of a courtship. Things were going well; Anastasia and I had been walking aimlessly for hours, though in reality that was only a delay tactic. We both knew the evening would end in the first kisses and caresses we were so eager for, which would play out in the semi-darkness of some calm plaza finally emptied of nosy kids and those ubiquitous retirees who employ the cheap trick of feeding pigeons in order to indulge their wanton voyeurism.

"You don't like soccer, do you?"

That's what Anastasia asked me. There was a sort of implicit plea in her voice, or at least I thought so.

"Of course not."

I lied instinctively, but also maybe out of habit. Anastasia, on the other hand, never lied. She was honest, perhaps unnecessarily so, which I found out for certain later but I began to sense that very night, when she told me all about her previous boyfriend, a sensational guy. They were twin souls: Both of them knew every Cure song by heart, even the ones they didn't like, because really they liked them all—some more than others, but they found them all beautiful. And also they could both recite long passages from *On Heroes and Tombs*, the novel by Ernesto Sabato, and they'd even taken a trip to Buenos Aires to experience, to re-create, to recover, to *live* that novel. But Anastasia had never been able to accept her boyfriend's interest—excessive, in her opinion—in soccer. At first she'd thought his exaggerated passion was a minor, reversible defect, but soon it became clear that he was a lost cause: he disappeared almost every weekend, and insisted on indoc-trinating Anastasia in the use of soccer metaphors, which she found irritating ("Your team has the ball," he'd intone, for example, instead of saying simply, "You choose"). Her boyfriend's love for soccer was neither the official nor the main reason for the end of that relationship, but it had played a role.

"Personally, I've always thought soccer was pretty stupid," I told her, with persuasive cynicism. "It's just nine idiots running around after a ball."

"Aren't there eleven? Eleven per team, so twenty-two?"

"To be honest, I have no idea," I went on, inspired. "I'm a Philistine when it comes to soccer. I've never even watched a show."

"You mean a match."

"Right, a match."

She looked at me as though I'd just said something amazing, and then she launched into a long and extraordinary harangue against soccer. Her words hurt me, partly because, stuck as I was with the character I'd just created, I couldn't disagree, and my neck started to hurt from so much nodding. I tried to distance myself by looking at her hair, newly dyed a color halfway between red and orange, and at her teeth, which were almost unrealistically white and small, and also very odd, because they seemed to have been arranged in pairs, with very visible gaps between one pair and another, as if she had taken them out and put them back in out of pure boredom.

Anastasia talked about sexism, nationalism, and barbarity, and her arguments all struck me as valid. Her position summarized what many of my teachers and peers thought about soccer, especially since violence in stadiums had become a subject of national conversation. Even I—after being spit on by a fan from a rival team and mugged by a hooligan from my own—had stopped going to the stadium.

Maybe during that time I also had a latent anti-soccer impulse that was tied to my social-climbing impulse, my desire to belong to that community of skeptical, critical, bullshitter intellectuals who held soccer in such contempt. (It was a little like what happened to me with music throughout adolescence: those times were not propitious for the eclecticism that's now so highly valued, and I had started out liking folk music and then moved on to thrash metal, new wave, punk, and then back to folk, with all the ensuing changes in dress, friends, and even habits.)

## VII.

Soon Anastasia and I managed to lose ourselves in conversations about Krzysztof Kieslowski's *The Double Life of Véronique* and his *Three Colors* trilogy, and we also assembled, with all the urgency of intense love, a soundtrack that even included a few—though certainly not all—Cure songs, as well as a broad swath of literary concurrences that excluded only *On Heroes and Tombs*, for obvious reasons. (I think I managed to convince her that *Abadón, the Exterminator* was better than *On Heroes and Tombs*, though I was never certain about that. Honestly, to this day, I couldn't say for sure if I like any of Sabato's books, except for *The Tunnel*, which isn't that good, though every Chilean kid who was into books went crazy for it around age twelve, and as such it possesses, for me, the indisputable status of a personal classic or guilty pleasure.)

I don't want to caricature my relationship with Anastasia. Well, not too much, anyway; sometimes it's inevitable and even advisable to caricature, since it allows us to forgive those people we once were. Though in reality the people we should forgive are the insensitive grown-ups we are today, so willing to minimize something that was—and we know this, but pretend not to—enormous and serious and wonderful. We talk about the past and laugh at ourselves as if, in the future, we will never laugh at who we are now. Anyway, I don't want to run on here: what I meant to say was that Anastasia and I very quickly built a relationship of absolute companionship and dizzying trust, and even so, I would not own up to my cowardly parallel romance with soccer.

## VIII.

One good thing about soccer sadness is how compatible it is with other forms of sadness. For example, those long afternoons when

Anastasia and I sprawled on the living room rug in religious silence to listen to Sarah Vaughan or Henryk Górecki: she would ruminate on her own personal tribulations, while I would endlessly rue some missed opportunity for a goal by Ivo Basay or Fernando Vergara or Tunga González.

## IX.

By the time the Chilean national team returned to the international contest to compete in the qualifiers for the 1998 World Cup in France, Anastasia and I were practically living together. I had to make up one excuse after another to watch the games, tucked away in some bar or ensconced in the cold sofa at my parents' house. But sometimes I simply couldn't manage to escape, and it was hard to fight back the bitterness I felt as Anastasia and I strolled through a deserted park, or maybe sat down to watch some extraordinary Fellini film, at the exact time when the whole country was cheering for our boys in red.

I can situate my worst memory in this regard precisely on the evening of November 16, 1997: seventy thousand fevered souls were packed into the National Stadium, excited about Chile's likely qualification for the World Cup, while Anastasia and I, a few blocks away, protected by the half darkness of the closed blinds, were trying to screw.

"What's going on out there?" I asked in medias res, when the crowd exploded with joy over the 1–0 score.

"I think there's a match," Anastasia told me. "Chile's playing, the national team, La Roja."

"Julián Zamorano must have scored," I said.

"*Iván* Zamorano," Anastasia corrected me.

"Right, that guy, Iván Zamorano."

My ruse was double, since I knew perfectly well that Zamorano was injured. So, while the Chilean players gave it their all on the pitch, we were inside listening to *OK Computer* on my auto-reverse tape deck. When I listen to that album now, I sometimes catch myself trying uselessly to remember exactly which Radiohead song was playing in my room when Chamuca Barrera took off on the miraculous solo run that culminated in an exquisite score, or when, a few minutes later, El Matador Salas made the game a little safer with his usual efficiency, or when Candonga Carreño headed the third goal toward the end of the match, ultimately ensuring our presence in the 1998 World Cup.

x.

A new soccer concept my son has recently introduced is the *self-foul*, a term that was spontaneously coined one day when he tried to kick the ball and fell over. That's exactly what my whole relationship with Anastasia was: the regrettable and prolonged result of an absurd self-foul.

I'll finish the story real quick:

One morning, while I was in the shower, Anastasia went through my drawers and found my Colo-Colo jersey. I should have gotten mad and asked her why she was rifling through my things, but I felt like I'd been caught red-handed. I explained that it had been a birthday present from my dad, and that in spite of our difficult relationship, the shirt had sentimental value. She remembered the Católica jersey her ex-boyfriend had given her, and we turned it into a joke. I should have seen that incident as a warning or a portent of what was to come.

"You know very well why," Anastasia told me a few weeks later when she broke up with me.

I've noticed that these days, instead of saying "terminó conmigo" (she broke up with me), people are saying "me terminó," or "she ended me." I think this new expression is great, because that's exactly what I felt: that she ended me, liquidated me, annihilated me. She took out my batteries, unplugged me, cut my cables, and stashed me away in a box in the attic forever. Later, thanks to the indiscretion of our mutual friends, I found out that my constant absences and excuses had made her conclude that I had a lover, or several. I had never cheated on her, but it was still hard for me to argue my case, because in fact I was leading a double life. I suffered over the breakup, I really did, especially when I found out from the same big-mouthed friends that she had a new boyfriend just two weeks later. I spent months insisting that we talk; I at least wanted to clarify things. It was hard to convince her to see me.

"My boyfriend is upstairs in my room," she told me, in an effort to humiliate me, on the day we finally did meet up.

"I just want you to know the truth," I said, and maybe I even imagined a drumroll before I came out with the next words, which must have sounded perfectly idiotic. "The thing is, I like soccer. I like soccer a lot. I've always liked it. Sometimes I even dream I'm scoring goals in stadiums full of people. Magnificent goals. That's the whole truth."

She looked at me in shock, the contempt frozen on her face. I went on talking about how much I liked soccer, and I assured her that all those times she'd thought I was cheating on her, I was actually watching a game, with friends or with my dad.

"With your dad? I thought you hadn't spoken to him in years!"

"That's what I told you, to throw you off. The truth is we don't talk much. We watch games and talk about them, that's all."

"That's the stupidest excuse you could have possibly come up with."

"But..."

Just then her brand-new boyfriend appeared in the living room and put an end to the visit.

I saw her boyfriend again many times after that; almost every week, I ran into him at the vegetable stand that sold rotten tomatoes and rancid lettuce where we both bought weed. I said hi to him, of course, I always say hi; he also greeted me, raising his eyebrows with a kind of happy indifference. Later I found out he was a fan of the U, but he was always wearing the shirt of a different soccer team: Real Madrid, A. C. Milan, Inter de Porto Alegre, San Lorenzo de Almagro. He was one of those global fans who were starting to appear at the time, the kind you can now find frequenting liquor stores, music festivals, and record shops. I have to admit he looked good in all those jerseys.

I learned my lesson, of course, or maybe my stupidity just took a different form over the years. Later, soccer stopped being, for me, a purely masculine avocation. Though I didn't deserve it, fate rewarded me with two female friends who were soccer fans and Colo-Colo addicts, thanks to whom I realized that soccer sadness is not at all exclusive to men. With them, I started going to matches again, first in the extraordinary years of Colo-Colo's four league championship wins under Claudio Borghi, and later to see the illustrious national team of Marcelo Bielsa and the golden generation of Arturo Vidal, Alexis Sánchez, Claudio Bravo, Mauricio Isla, et al.

I started to spend more time away from Chile, and although soccer never stopped being of the utmost importance to me, I started watching it almost exclusively on television, and alone. I even picked up the habit of watching matches while riding a stationary bike, as though playing a kind of Nintendo Wii. Sometimes I still do this: if Pibe Solari has to make a run to break through the back line, I pedal faster but when Colorado Gil or Vicente Pizarro start trying to run out the clock, I slow down.

\*　\*　\*

## XI.

Of all the programs on TV, soccer is the only one not governed by the imperatives of information or entertainment. Commentators and pundits can spend the full ninety minutes of a game talking about how bad or deficient or boring it is, and it never even occurs to them that they could lose their viewers, because in fact that possibility does not exist. Those who watch the game are a faithful, captive audience, and we'll stay right there, hypnotized, or, in the worst case, lulled to sleep by the lack of action. And not even our own snores—or the suspicion that the game remained every bit as boring during the minutes we were dozing—will make us change the channel or turn off the TV.

There's a certain beauty in these scenes of honest, sober boredom. But TV broadcasts are always a little redundant anyway. Radio commentators are poets who leap from metaphor to metaphor with admirable speed, or else they're skilled classical storytellers with recognizable and even study-able styles, able to *make the unknown known* through just a couple of brushstrokes. TV commentators, meanwhile, are condemned to repeat what we're already watching with our own two eyes, telling a story we already know. It's a difficult profession, though perhaps the hardest job is that of the pundits, with whom we are rarely in agreement. Except when they are retired players whom we've loved or respected, pundits always receive our invariable, perhaps excessive and unfair contempt.

I felt that way especially about the sports journalist Felipe Bianchi: I always disagreed with his game analysis, and even when I agreed, I invented some nuance to nitpick. Later, through a series of random coincidences, I had the privilege of getting to know him well: he turned out to be a very nice guy, compassionate, generous, and unexpectedly shy, not to mention a good father and reader—of Rubem Fonseca, Nick Hornby, Pedro Lemebel—and the creator of

ALEJANDRO ZAMBRA

innovative salads and unforgettable cocktails. Once we were friends, whenever I saw him reviewing a game or digging into debates on the news, I tried to recite that list of virtues, but it was no good: I still couldn't stand him. And that was in the years of Bielsa and Jorge Sampaoli, when the national team almost always won.

I'm recounting all this to get to the point when, thanks to another series of flukes, Felipe and I were both living in New York, and we would get together to watch Chile play in the Centennial Copa América, now commentated on and analyzed by others. There's nothing better than watching the game with a dear friend, both of us very nervous: We'd have a drink, snack on a cheese plate, turn on the TV, all as it should be. But from time to time Felipe would come out with some comment that was, of course, pertinent and intelligent, and I couldn't help but contradict him. And sometimes, at the risk of being impolite, it was very hard for me not to take advantage of the opportunity to shush the pundit, even if he wasn't a pundit anymore, but rather a faithful friend who showed up with Belgian beer and strange, fantastic cigarettes. In spite of his famous fierceness and his well-earned reputation as a polemicist, Felipe, oddly, accepted my criticism and my bad manners. Maybe he recognized in me the same impulse that had led him to become a sports pundit: the urge to silence the sports pundit.

XII.

My arrival in Mexico more or less coincided with Matías Fernández's arrival to Necaxa, which I took as an eloquent sign of benevolence from Our Lord Jesus Christ. During the year and a half that Mati played here, I followed his dignified campaign as faithfully as always, and when he left I really did try to keep liking Necaxa, but soon I had to accept that I was watching the games without much interest, or with the average level of interest I feel watching any match in any league from any other country in the world but Chile.

The Mexican league is superior to the Chilean one in almost every sense, but once you get to a certain age—in my case, forty-two—it's impossible to get excited about any soccer but your own. Soccer is more idiosyncratic than we tend to think. If there's a game on between the Pumas and the Chivas de Guadalajara, I'll watch it, but if at the same time, say, Ñublense is playing Antofagasta, I won't hesitate to tune in to the Chilean league. Maybe it's comforting just to know that what I'm watching on the computer screen is happening right then in Chile. Or maybe deep down I still want to memorize the lineups of all the teams in the Chilean league. Maybe someday, if my son gets interested in the sport, I'll finally take to Mexican soccer. But I don't even know if I want my son to like soccer.

## XIII.

During my son's first two years of life, I missed a whole lot of games—nearly all of them. The part of me that wanted nothing more than to turn on the TV and watch soccer with my baby in my arms always lost by a shutout to the part of me that changed his diapers or sang him lullabies or took him for walks in the stroller through Parque España. A little over a year ago, though, Colo-Colo's terrible season led me to negotiate parenting shifts with my wife far in advance, so that I could witness it in real time as my team either salvaged their dignity or went to shit. Colo-Colo could stop being a big team, which perhaps would have had its advantages, but of course the possibility made us fans suffer as never before.

After one of those horrible games, my son peered at me the way you look at someone who seems distracted or absent.

"I'm sad, because Colo-Colo lost and they're going to move down to the second division," I explained.

The words were more or less incomprehensible to him, but they stuck with him anyway. He got into the habit of telling me—delightfully, exaggeratedly imitating the tone I use to console him—not to worry, that everything would be all right, that very soon Colo-Colo would start winning again, with goals scored by John Lennon, Frida Kahlo, and Batman and Robin Hood. (I haven't wanted to clear up his confusion there; maybe the world would be less unfair if instead of that good-for-nothing Robin, Batman's sidekick were Robin Hood.)

Just as my literary vocation is related to soccer, my son's tentative soccer education has, in a way, a literary origin. One morning it occurred to me to have him listen to Mauricio Redolés's album *Bailables de Cueto Road*, which features the narration of an invented soccer match between Chile's living and dead poets. The dead poets win 8–2, thanks to an excellent performance by Jorge Teillier, making his first start. Listening to Redolés, I was able to recover my passion for commentating, giving play-by-plays of other equally unreal games for my son: Sea Animals versus Land Animals, Dinosaurs versus Non-Dinosaurs, the Beatles versus Los Bunkers (a five-a-side game, I guess), Fingers versus Trees and Flowers, Months versus Chilean Volcanoes, and so on.

Up till then my son had considered the ball to be just another toy—one with a curiously round shape, but a toy nonetheless—and he insisted on keeping it in his basket of stuffed animals. But those play-by-plays and the new words and narrative forms associated with them made him start to find meaning in the game. And thus began some very strange pickup games on our patio, matches in which my son enjoyed the play-by-plays more than the game itself, or maybe the game consisted of saying and making me say words like *nutmeg*, *screamer*, *panenka*, or *toe poke*, or of conjugating new verbs like *shimmy*, *dribble*, and *volley*, or of employing formulas like *yours*, *mine*, *to you*, *to me* (classic stock phrases of my dear Mimica), or of chanting, "Don't say 'goal'; say 'golazo'" (in our version, the phrase becomes eternal because *golazo* turns into *golazazo* and *golazazazo* and so on).

The only time we've watched a game together—a particularly bad one, the final of the 2021 European Championship between Italy and England—my son started out very excited, jumping on the bed and cheering all the players' movements in bursts of his newly acquired verbal exuberance. But after about fifteen minutes, he went quiet and whispered into my ear in the beautiful tone of a secret, as he does when he wants to emphasize that he's speaking seriously:

"Dad, I don't really understand soccer that much. What's happening?"

It was a boring game, that was all, I explained. I didn't want to tell him that the vast majority of games are every bit as boring as that one.

## XIV.

"Why'd you name her Anastasia?" my wife asks.

It takes me a few seconds to realize she thinks Anastasia wasn't real, that I'm making her up.

"Because that was her name."

"Really? Like the Russian princess?"

"Right," I tell her.

"I thought she was a metaphor."

"For what?"

"For me."

\*   \*   \*

She says she likes my story. I tell her it's an essay. She says she likes my essay, in a tone that makes it clear she thinks it's a story and she doesn't much like it. I ask her what it is she doesn't like. She tells me she does like it, especially some of the jokes. She says she doesn't understand all the jokes, but she understands that they are jokes. She recommends that I lie and say I've become a fan of women's soccer. I tell her it wouldn't be a lie, because in fact I followed the entire campaign of the Chilean women's team in the 2019 World Cup.

"Name five players."

"Christiane Endler, Carla Guerrero, Javiera Toro, Francisca Lara, María José Rojas, Yessenia López, Rosario Balmaceda..."

She thinks I'm making the names up. I tell her all about the anguished elimination, Francisca Lara's penalty against the crossbar that could have been the 3–0 that would have meant moving on to the last sixteen.


We get into the car, my wife at the wheel, thoughtful, while I ride in the back with our son. Lately, he's has been getting mad when he feels left out of a conversation ("Don't talk to each other!" he implores us), but now he is listening attentively, as if trying to understand our debate from a philosophical point of view. But maybe he's not listening. He's looking out at the trees, and maybe that's what he is trying to understand or decipher or absorb: the enigma of some trees that move their branches in the breeze as though waving or begging for mercy. Or the atmosphere of the street corner crowded with flexible jugglers and insistent window washers where we wait with obligatory patience for the length of a long red light.

"Talk about women's soccer, but really you should focus on the violence of the sport, about the economic interests of corporations, about the absurd competitiveness of those macho men. You can get all that in if you develop Estefanía's arguments more."

"Anastasia," I correct her.

"But Estefanía is a prettier name."

"But her name was Anastasia."

"Well, make Anastasia more consistent. I don't really believe in her as a character. Make her more serious."

"But that's how she was. And she *is* a serious character, it seems to me."

"Make her more serious."

"But my story isn't that serious."

"Your essay."

"My essay isn't serious. Or it is. Really, it's very serious. Sadness is a very serious subject."

Aside from a hipster uncle who likes to go around the city in his Barcelona jersey, everyone in my wife's family, including her, claims to be fans of the Pumas from UNAM, the university they all went to. But it seems like my son has caught on to the fact that to them, soccer isn't very important or interesting. When my wife was little, there was one morning on her school playground when she was hit in the face by three consecutive balls. Since then, she has associated soccer solely with the possibility of getting hit, and as such she stays cautiously on the sidelines of our pickup games.

"Have you finished your essay?" she asks me later that night as she tries to play "Despacito" on the ukulele.

"I'm missing the end, but I'm not going to write it yet."

"Why not?"

"I'll write it in a couple of weeks, once we know whether Chile is going to the World Cup in Qatar."

"Hopefully they don't go, Qatar is a terrible country for women. Is Mexico going?"

"Mexico always goes," I tell her. "It's easy for them, the Concacaf qualifiers are..."

"But didn't we lose to Chile seven–nil?"

"Yeah, but that was five years ago. Now everything has changed," I tell her, downcast.

## XV.

I'm writing these final lines on my phone while my son is in his soccer class. That was his mother's idea—she says she doesn't want the kid to go around with a perpetual fear of stray soccer balls. In today's class there are five girls and three boys, including my son. It's the first time they've been allowed to play without masks, so I'm finally seeing their faces, their big smiles, although at times they turn serious, focused on the instructions of a sweet, energetic coach, a woman in her thirties who is wearing an official Pumas shirt. The class follows a system of gradual assimilation, so for now it seems like anything but a soccer class: they play ring-around-the-rosy and hide-and-seek; they jump in and out of Hula Hoops; they run around without order or coherence while waving ribbons (I've tried to figure out what exactly this game consists of, and apparently it's just that: running chaotically, freely, joyfully, while waving those ribbons). There are a couple of goals, but they're used only for taking shelter from an imaginary storm (when the rain is real, of course, class is canceled). There are also soccer balls—the field is covered with lightweight, colorful balls, which the kids kick happily, straight to any which way.

While I watch them run and jump, heedless of any idea of competition, I think about when I used take classes at the Cobresal Soccer School, Maipú branch, where I stood out as one of the subs with the least chance of ever starting. I guess the coaches tried not to destroy our dreams too early on, but there was no way they would give me more than two or three minutes at the end of each game. That's why to this day I identify with the players who come on during injury time, just to run down the clock. I used to go home devastated, ruminating on the defeat in silence—not the team's defeat, but mine alone, and I always told my parents that I'd done well, that I was sure I'd get to start any day now.

But that was a different kind of soccer sadness, of course, which will be the subject of another essay or another story. As for our fathers' soccer sadness—so different from but at times so similar to the soccer sadness felt by those of us who are now fathers, and who, as such, attend to the constant re-creation of our own childhoods—as for that sadness, after re-reading these pages, I have to admit I have been unfair. Because that sadness was, in reality, the absence of extra happiness. Our fathers were sad—of course they were, every minute of every hour of all the days of their lives they were sad—but a win was a respite, a palliative, a courtesy, a treat; it was a measly, momentary reprieve during which things didn't seem so terrible. Plus, their soccer sadness humanized them, proved they were fallible and childish, just like we were back then, like we are now.


Oh, right: last night Chile lost, and they won't be going to the World Cup. Everyone saw it; everyone knows. I'm not going to talk about that now. I just don't want to talk about that right now.

# SPIRITUALITY

*by* HALLIE GAYLE

COLIN AND HIS MOTHER visited the Baptist church all the way out in Hillsboro on the day he got glasses. His second-grade teacher thought he had a learning disability, but it turned out he was severely near-sighted and that's why he couldn't sit still at his desk. They drove an hour to get his eyes checked at Walmart because his mother had some cousin, Yolene, who would be giving him the exam and glasses for free. He put on the round glasses and followed Yolene and his mother up to the register, where they stood talking and laughing for a long time. He wanted to take them off. Back in the parking lot, his mother was holding him by the arm, pulling him to their car, and when he took off the glasses, she yanked him and said, "Don't you want to see?"

A scrawny teenager in an orange vest was pushing a train of blue carts, and when Colin put his glasses on again, the blue was sharp and pulsing, the teenager's face red and wrecked. But before that day he didn't even know the world was all blurry. He pressed the glasses to his nose and looked at his mother, who by that point was standing by their car with her hand on her hip. He could see that her lipstick was smeared at the edges, that she still had some black dye stains around her temples from last night's over-the-sink treatment.

They did not get back on the highway that day and instead just drove fast down a road, passing a field of sunflowers, a graveyard, big green acres of nothing. They came upon a small church, and his mother drove right on over the grass and parked under the giant crooked arms of an oak tree. "Colin," his mother said after she got out of the car, lit a cigarette, and started pulling her hair up into a scrunchie. "This is where I used to come when I was a girl, with Grandma Jace. After Daddy drove over that woman's foot."

There were only about ten people total inside the church, clustered in the front-row pews. The people turned around and nodded, then went right on back to listening to the sermon as if it was no big deal that Colin and his mother had come in after the service had already started. They squeezed into an empty seat at the very end of one of the front pews, Colin's mother putting her arm across him like a seat belt.

The preacher was a very fat man. He was telling a story about how in the first part of his life, he didn't know how to read. All his life his teachers were trying to teach him how to read but the letters didn't work right in his brain. Then one day when he was in his later teens, the preacher opened up the Bible and he could read. He opened up the Bible right to the Blessitudes: Blessed are those who are mentally troubled. Blessed are all the children. Blessed are the mothers trying to stretch a dollar.

Maybe his mind didn't want to absorb anything else but the good news, is what the preacher declared.

A woman who his mother later said looked like a meth addict came and played the piano. She was not very good at it, but the fat preacher began singing, and so the ten or so other people stood up and sang too. To the left of Colin was a man with stubby gray fingers who smelled like cow dung. Half his shirt was untucked, and he was swaying from boot to boot as he listened to the singing. Diagonally in front of them was an old lady with thin pink curls who clutched the arm of another lady with a severe underbite. Next to her, a woman in a hoodie held her head cocked to the side, tears brimming in her skunk eyes. Colin was wearing his glasses, and everything was vibrant. The stage had maroon carpet; the piano was a smooth honey brown; there was a window behind the stage that was red, green, blue, and yellow—all the pieces of glass making up a picture of Jesus rising out of the water. The preacher was not on the stage or behind the pulpit but on the floor to the side, and he just stood there and sang with tears rolling down his peach-colored cheeks, and for some reason that made Colin start crying too.

His mother leaned against the bench in front of them with her head down. She was popping her jaw by rotating it in a circle, and he tried not to look at her. After the sermon, she took Colin by the hand and marched him right up to the preacher and said, "I think the Holy Spirit is knocking on the door of his heart." He didn't realize she had seen him crying. His mother had never, ever taken him by the hand like that before, and he didn't even know she was a believer in the Holy Spirit. He stood in front of the big-bellied preacher, who was like Santa Claus, only warmer, because he had sandy-blond hair and a green shirt with sweat under the armpits and around each of the buttons. While his mother went outside to smoke with some woman she knew from way back in her childhood, Colin and the preacher sat at a table in a sunlit kitchen in the back. All the other church people ate sweet pastries and drank coffee at the foldout tables around them. And the preacher, who had learned earlier from his mother that she was without a husband, said, "Boy, Jesus will be your daddy. If you need something, you just call on Him." He winked and then pulled out these pens from the pocket of his shirt. He had about three pens, and they were not the normal kind of pen, but wooden. He wobbled over to a storage closet in the kitchen and came back holding a box in his hands. The box said SUPERIOR CIGARS, and there was a woman on it, wearing a polka-dot bikini, a piece of grass between her teeth. "Here are my pens, Colin. I carve them out of wood." The pens were different colors—turquoise, dark red, a white one with a black stripe down the side. He gave Colin a solid brown pen, but later, his mother used it to stab one of her boyfriends in the throat. Some weeks later, when they were just moving into apartment 46. This boyfriend had a tattoo of Frankenstein looking in the mirror stretched across his hairy back, and he would come over and walk around in his underwear. His mother was always saying, "Just for tonight," but then it would be days and the man didn't leave.

Colin didn't see her stab him, but he heard the boyfriend scream, "You fucking crazy bitch!" When Colin ran out of the bedroom to see what was going on, the man was holding his hand over his throat, and in the middle of the living room, there was the preacher's wooden pen, the spring popped out, the white stick of ink detached from it like a tiny bone.

They went back to that church only one other time—not much longer after the stabbing incident. The preacher got his mother's number from Yolene. He must have had what his mother called "a six sense," because he called her one day when they had just come home from job hunting all day in the June heat—Colin waiting in the car or on a bench by a trash can, his mother going to each and every store in all the shopping strips of H.E.B., application in hand. His mother wore black pants and a blue button-up that day. When the preacher called, she tore off her shirt and was sitting in her bra on the arm of their couch, a sunburn on her face, her head nodding and her eyes closed. The following Sunday, they drove all the way back to Hillsboro, and his mother wore a long yellow dress with her hair brushed back into a bun. "They're going to pray over me," she said, looking down at Colin as if to make sure he understood. She wore her green heart-shaped sunglasses, drove ninety down 35, and didn't bother with the radio.

The preacher was taking prayer requests. One by one the people in the pews raised their hands. A young lady reported that their family's German shepherd had died of heartworms. The woman behind her needed a blessing for her husband, who was getting a colonoscopy the following Wednesday. Another woman—sitting in the back next to a man in a cowboy hat who looked like he was wanting to leave— needed prayers for her daughter Amity, who was back in rehab. The preacher stood in front of everyone and listened to the requests from all the people, nodding and rubbing his thumbs together against his big belly. Colin's mother was not raising her hand, but the preacher called on her anyway. When he asked her what load we can all pass on to the good, good Lord, she was leaning her skinny body against the pew in front of her, gripping it with her hands. This time, it was she who was crying.

The preacher then said: "Why don't you come on up here. Come on up. Everyone in this room here, we love you."

His mother kneeled on the steps of the stage and everyone gathered around and placed a hand on her. Colin stood back from the huddle of church people, and the piano player, who was at her piano, gave him a flat missing-tooth smile and hit a few notes.

When they were leaving, the preacher came toward Colin with his arms out to hug him. But the preacher tripped on the cord of the electric fan by the entrance and fell right on top of Colin. Colin could not breathe under the smashing weight of him, felt that maybe if the Holy Spirit was knocking on the door of his heart, that was the moment he exited. Two old ladies who smelled like Kleenex came and picked him up and took him outside and let him wail. "Let it out, boy," they kept saying, rubbing his back. "Let it out."

On the way back home, his mother popped two sticks of cinnamon gum into her mouth and said, "I don't actually believe in a god, Colin. Those people are kind. Kind people, but whack." And when they were close to home, a police car turned on its siren and flashing red lights behind them and signaled them to pull off onto the shoulder of the highway. The officer walked on up to their car, came over to his mother's window, and wrote them up a speeding ticket.

They were no longer living in a hotel. No longer living with Lennette, the woman who had an olive green freezer stocked with three kinds of ice cream and little plants in tin cans lined up beside her balcony door. No longer living with "what's-his-name," who had a pool table but hardly any furniture. Not living with those women in the neighborhood off Eastchase, who gathered on the wraparound couch late at night after their shifts, those mean women who sucked smoke from colorful glass bongs, white clouds coming from their mouths between all their yelling. Not living with his mother's cousin who had a hot tub in his garage with a poster right in front of it of a girl in an American flag bikini, a thick yellow snake draped over her neck and arms and held out in her palms.

They were living in apartment 46. They had a bed next to a window that looked out at a cottonwood. They got a couch for free from a widower on Craigslist who was moving to the coast "to start all over from scratch." A light gray couch that his mother said was the color of repression, so she put an orange tie-dyed spread over it, tucking the bright fabric into the edges. She also came home one day with two plastic bags full of these tall green prayer candles. The candles had pictures of flying dollar bills glued to their glass cases. She set them on the window ledge, on the coffee table, in the kitchen by the sink. "The money gods," she told Colin, "are the only gods worth praying to."

When Colin's mother finally got a callback for a job one evening, she wanted to celebrate, so they walked a few blocks to get snow cones. They sat on a concrete bench in the weedy lot of Ed's Snow-Balls, scooping syrupy rainbow ice into their mouths with little plastic spoons. A small broken moon in a big fresh sky, summer air buzzing with all the cicadas. "It's gonna be different from now on, you hear me, Colin?" He dug his head into the side of her waist, took her long arm and held it out in front of him with both his hands, planting kisses from her middle finger all the way up to her shoulder.

She had landed two jobs, one in the middle of the day and one in the evening. Three nights a week, in the evenings, she worked the night shift at a restaurant all the way downtown. A lady named Lucia in apartment 49 came over and slept on their couch, since Lucia worked all day, too, and she told Colin to wake her up if anything bad happened, an emergency. But sometimes Lucia couldn't sleep, and they watched action movies together on channel 57 while she painted her nails. "Yo, Colin," she would say. "You think this color brings out my eyes?" She'd press her hand to the coffee table and let Colin run the little brush of bright paint over each nail. Colin would hold his breath and try not to get the paint on her skin. He liked when she stayed up because sometimes she would fart, a loud vibrating fart, and she'd say, "Pew, Colin, why you farting?" And Colin would laugh and laugh and hit her on the shoulder and say, "No, that's you, Lucia, that's you!"

He'd fall asleep on the couch next to Lucia, sometimes pressed against her big tits. He would wake up when his mother came home late in her bright yellow shirt with the hard, red letters, her black apron still on, as if she had run out the door in the middle of taking someone's order.

In the daytime, his mother had some kind of job where she typed forms into a computer at an auto-repair shop, and she had to look nice. That's what she said when they went to Goodwill and she filled her arms with work slacks and pencil skirts. "You think people will take me seriously in these?" his mother asked when they were in the dressing room, as Colin sat on the floor in a pile of clothes, peeking through the crack into the stall next to theirs. In there was another woman, naked, picking up the big rolls of her belly with her hands. When the woman's eyes met Colin's gaze, he thought he was in trouble, but the woman just gave him a little wink.

While his mother was at the auto shop, Colin stayed with a woman named Sue. Sue lived in a long house on Brown Trail that was very dark inside because it was surrounded by trees and no light could get in. There were about five other neighborhood kids that also stayed there, and they were always either throwing baby dolls around in the backyard for Sue's wiener dog, Macy Louise, or they were all sprawled out in the dark living room, watching something on the television. He once wet his pants on the ugly green carpet because he didn't want to use the bathroom. In Sue's bathroom were four boxes of cat litter, lined up against the bathtub. The tub must not have been used, because there wasn't even a shower curtain, and inside of it was the type of chair that had a glass bowl attached to the top, the kind of chair women sat in at salons with foil folded all up in their hair. It wasn't the cat litter or the big, awkward chair that scared Colin, but the knitted dummy slouched in the seat. The dummy had no face but had yellow yarn for hair. She wore a light purple dress on top of a red-and-white-striped turtleneck. When he tried to pee, he was afraid the dummy would come and put her arms around him and try and snatch at his penis.

\* \* \*

On Sundays, Colin's mother was off. On Sundays she pulled the blinds up to let the warm afternoon light in. They made a path with all the pillows they owned, from the door of their apartment all the way to the end of the hall. Colin's mother turned up her stereo as loud as it could go. They jumped from one pillow to the next, throwing their arms in the air. His mother twisted her dark hair up on top of her head. She wore her big, baggy T-shirts with the funny sayings on them; Colin in nothing but his underwear.

The other time he got to be alone with his mother was in the mornings. She would put him in the bathtub. And because they were living in apartment 46, there was no one knocking on the door because they needed to pee or do their hair or brush their teeth.

One morning Colin was smearing bubbles on the ledge of the tub and against the tiled wall. He was watching his mother prepare for work. His mother was smoking a cigarette and drinking her coffee and listening to a radio program where a woman preacher named Janelle Jackson talked about the fierce love of Jesus Christ: "It ain't a weak kind of love. A kind of love that makes a generation of posers. It's a love that brings you to your knees. Your knees."

In the steam from the bath and all her cigarette smoke, she was clamping her eyelashes in an eyelash curler, listening to Janelle's passionate shouting: "I'm worshiping a God of compassion. A God who gets on the level of my grief. A God not on a throne looking down at me but holding me here in my pain." His mother dropped the curler into the sink and leaned against the counter and shut her eyes, a big long tear making its way through her powdered cheek. This is how he knew that his mother, deep down, was still what the preacher had called "a born-again believer." The program was only twenty minutes, and as soon as the music started up, she jabbed the orange OFF button with her long finger and wiped her cheek.

She was listening to Janelle Jackson's program, LET'S GET REAL, every morning, but after some time that station wasn't coming in clearly, even though his mother was moving the antenna back and forth, holding it in place at the bottom with tinfoil. She tried plugging the small stereo into different outlets in the apartment, carrying it in her arms from room to room. "Motherfucker," she mumbled as she turned the black dial back and forth, as Janelle's voice was lost in all the static, then in some kind of rap music. It made Colin think it was like someone screaming out in the ocean.

Time went by and his mother wasn't waking up early for her job, and she hadn't said anything about it, but she must have been fired. This is what happened when she worked at Kroger a few years back. She'd gotten fired for eating doughnuts. Colin had pictured his mother sitting up on the table where all the bread was displayed, dipping her hands into the glass case where the baked goods were kept, doughnut flakes falling all down her Kroger uniform, sticking around her mouth.

Another bad thing happened when she was driving home from her restaurant job downtown. His mother had seen some kind of dark figure in the middle of her lane and swerved the car right into the median wall of the highway. She came home that night with her face intense and shining like the moon. Her makeup was smeared against her cheekbones, her round eyes hard and black. His mother had gotten on her knees to explain it to him. "The car blew up, Colin. We don't have a car anymore." He imagined her circling the explosion, hitting the crushed-up hood and leaning against it in surrender, smoke rising, her skinny arms held around her rib cage. In his mind, Colin could see her standing there on the side of the highway with her hair all wild in the lights of passing cars, slouching there in that way that made people think she was a young girl.

Colin didn't know how she was getting home, but about a week later he heard the name Ron Green. His mother had a best friend named Clarissa. Clarissa would come over with her five-year-old girl, Tracy, on afternoons when his mother was off.

"Get the fuck off me," Clarissa said to Tracy one day as she walked through the door. She stood in the middle of the living room with big spider lashes and eyes painted with little wings, with these sandals that wrapped all the way up her ankles. She wore cutoff overalls and a sports bra, and there was writing all over her left thigh, cursive tattoos that Colin wished he could read. On her hip was Tracy, who had something sticky around her tiny pink lips, and long, stringy hair that was falling out of a braid. Clarissa peeled her daughter off her. "Go play with Colin." Tracy shook her head no and clung to her mom's leg, and Clarissa whispered in her ear, "Remember, be good and we'll go to Toys R Us and you can pick out your prize."

"Two prizes," Tracy said.

"Fine, two prizes." Clarissa stuck out her tongue and made her eyes wide and silly.

Tracy kissed her mother right on the stomach, then ran to the couch and fell into it belly-first.

Clarissa and Colin's mom sat down in a square patch of sunlight by the window. They sat there with their knees up, passing a bottle of red wine that they took turns taking big gulps out of.

That's when his mother told Clarissa about Ron Green. One night she had missed the bus and was walking home in the dark, hitchhiking, phone dead, no goddamn coat. "He asked me how old I was, and I said take a guess. He said fifteen and I said, 'I've already had a baby and lived in eighteen different homes.' Then he asked me how I know it's eighteen and I said because I wrote it down, every home I ever lived in." Clarissa just sat there blinking; both of them were glowing in the orange light. Colin was on the couch with Tracy. They were watching a movie about giant ants and she had a rattle in her throat like she needed to cough, a big bubble of snot moving up and down as she breathed. "Anyway, we had a deep conversation about home, what is home. I told him how I don't even have a car and he said, 'You seem like a woman who has really lived a life.' I said, 'Yeah, I know a thing or two.'"

"So when did y'all have sex?"

"Oh, please, it's not like that. He's an old man! Plus… he's *married*."

Clarissa put up her hand and smiled at the floor.

His mother continued. "But he's been there every night, waiting for me in the parking lot when I get off. He asks me questions about my life. Sometimes he doesn't even get on the highway. We take the back way, and he stops the car over by some field and rolls down the window and we smoke. He said his wife doesn't like it when he smokes. He lives all the way out near Dallas but drives all the way over to Fort Worth for work. He told me he's lonely. He said, 'You ever wake up and realize there's a part of you, like a room inside of a house you forgot all about? And you go inside that room and realize the real you's been hiding there, sitting in trash, just watching static on a TV set like a ghost?'"

"He's not going to love you," Clarissa said.

"You don't know that," his mother shot back and stared out the window, hugging her knees.

"Well, I gotta go, baby. Fucking Ryan is coming for Tracy today. Then I'll be free all weekend."

His mother lay down on the carpet and closed her eyes. "You really think he's not going to love me?"

"All you do is drive around. He hasn't taken you on a date yet or anything."

\* \* \*

When Ron Green came into the picture, sometimes she didn't get home until the morning, and there was this pain in his chest when he bolted up in the middle of the night and his mother was not there, snoring next to him. What it felt like was a hand being slapped in a door. "Mama," he said about a million times, when they walked to the grocery store one morning, Colin tugging at her shirt as they went right on by the Quickway Market, started wandering through all these parking lots like she forgot where they had set off to. She took a chair from a dumpster and brought it back to their small balcony, which was not really a balcony but a small block of concrete with a flowerpot filled with her cigarette butts. She sat there wearing two coats and chain-smoked—sat there like her spine was broken.

Another morning she was rubbing him on the leg, trying to wake him up. She threw some things in Colin's backpack: his pajamas, a toothbrush. She walked him to the yellow apartments behind the warehouses on Harwood. Clarissa opened the door wearing a long brown dress, and Colin could see the hugeness of her breasts, long and heavy under the thin fabric, bulging out of the drooping armpit holes. She had no makeup on and could barely open her eyes as she listened to Colin's mother beg, say it would just be a weekend. "Um, no." Clarissa stepped outside and shut the door behind her. The TV was on at a loud volume. "No ma'am." She crinkled up her face and pushed his mother once, then twice. Then kept pushing and pushing until his mother was leaning up against the second-floor railing. "Come on, Raylene. Use your brain!" Clarissa shouted, pinning his mother to the railing. Right in front of them, the neighbor had his door open. The neighbor was watching TV and eating a big slice of pizza, but he was not looking at the TV; he was looking at Colin's mother and Clarissa, staring at them like a bored cow.

Clarissa was holding his mother in her arms, and Colin didn't know if she was wanting to hug her tight or strangle her. But his mother gave her some money wrapped up in a purple rubber band, pushed the wad right into her friend's chest.

Colin spent that weekend in Clarissa's waterbed with her and Tracy. "It's my first weekend off in fifteen days so I don't want to hear it," Clarissa said when Tracy cried because she couldn't go swing on the swings at Redbud Park. Clarissa wore a purple face mask and painted her toenails, smoked weed and drank white wine and watched reality-TV shows—*bleep* this and *bleep* that all through the apartment.

"I'm bored," Colin muttered as he tried to get comfortable on the wide, jiggling waterbed. Clarissa stared at him with her purple face full of dried-up cracks. "Your mama has issues," she said, bringing her wine to her lips, alternating with her joint that sat sizzling in a small copper bowl. She blew long curls of smoke off to her side. "Just you wait, Colin boy. She'll wake up eventually."

His mother picked him up on Sunday night. She had gotten a suntan. She must have went far away, because in Texas it was still winter. She was wearing a new coat. When they were back in their apartment, she shook dirty clothes out of a suitcase and handed Colin a jar of sand, a little seashell inside it. "You don't like it?"

Later that week she returned in the morning, right when the sun was coming up. Colin heard the door slam and his mother crying hysterically. He did not want to go out and see what was going on, but after some time hiding under the sheets, sweating and listening to his mother cry, he went out into the living room and saw her crawling on the floor, spit hanging from her mouth. She looked right at him, but it was like her weeping was making her blind. She was knocking things down with her hands: weeks-old beer cans spilling onto the carpet, the green candles, the jar of sand. She bit the orange tie-dye sheet like a dog and screamed with the cloth bunched up in her mouth and dragged it from the couch. She lay there on the floor with her butt in the air, her face smashed into the carpet. "Fuck this life!" she kept screaming. "Fuck this fucking life!"

At the clinic two weeks later, they found out about baby girl. His mother had told him that she was getting a procedure. She sat Colin down in a chair and told the nurse that Colin's daddy was working, and he wondered if she meant Ron. Ron Green. His mother lay back in a big tan chair. The nurse moved a lever to make it fall back. The nurse had given Colin a green sucker. He sat in his chair and sucked it until hard emerald flakes crushed on his tongue, his mouth growing green and sticky. His mother was very quiet and stared up at the ceiling. The room was dark with only the lights from the machine in the center of the room. The nurse wore purple scrubs and her brown hair was pulled tight into a ponytail, and her forehead was smooth and shiny, even in the dark. She was saying things to his mother, but his mother only stared straight up at the ceiling and didn't respond. The nurse parted the cloth that his mother had put on and rubbed some jelly all over her belly. "Gonna be kind of cold." She took a wand from the machine and moved it around. Colin stared at the machine over the lump of his mother. The screen was gray with swirly mounds, and then they could hear a thumping and the nurse said it was the heartbeat. It was the quietest quiet Colin had ever heard, with baby girl's heartbeat beating there and his mother on her back staring up at the ceiling. "My, oh my, it's a girl, don't you want to look?" And his mother shook her head, and even in the dark, he could see tears melting down the side of her face. They went to a restaurant in the same parking lot as the clinic. They sat in a booth with tall brown seats and his mother drank beer. She looked in her purse for her pack of cigarettes but didn't have them. On a kids' menu the waitress had given him, Colin colored a horse that was wearing a big sombrero, and his mother was staring straight ahead. He leaned into her and said, "It's a girl," and she said, "No, Colin, it's not anything. Tomorrow there won't be anything."

The next day his mother's alarm kept going off and she slept until two. And later, when the sun was already going down, they walked to Lone Star Wash and Dry and ran into Clarissa. Clarissa and his mother sat on top of the washing machines and talked in whispers that Colin could still hear: "It's inside me, swimming. A little dolphin girl. A baby girl, a fucking girl. Clarissa, I couldn't go through with it. I want her. Is that crazy?" Clarissa grabbed his mother by the chin and said, "You careless little ho, I swear to god." And they burst into hard, crackling laughter.


His mother leaned back and pulled a bright bedsheet—lime green with pink Hawaiian flowers—from someone else's basket that was sitting on the machines behind them. She shook the sheet open and pulled it over her and Clarissa. They were there under the fort of the sheet for a long time. Colin was on the floor with Tracy, the two of them flicking a quarter back and forth. Tracy climbed into his lap and put her chubby arms around his neck. She let her fingers climb his face and that's when she pulled off his glasses. The glasses spun off and slid under one of the dryers, and when Colin stood up, all he could see was the blurry green and pink, wavering.


The next morning he was starving. He was so hungry his rib cage ached, and it made him start crying. He wandered out into the living room with a blanket over his head and sat down in the middle of the carpet and everything broke open in him. A big rush of need came out through his mouth in vibrating wails that shook his whole body in the sticky shards of morning sun. He rarely cried, but when he did, he couldn't stop. Under the blanket he started to sweat and scream.

"Jesus Christ," his mother said, walking out from the bedroom, rubbing her eyes. She was wearing her bright yellow sweatpants that said JUICY down the side. She was going through all the cabinets, all of them, slamming them. Opening the fridge and shutting it, then opening it again as if something would magically appear in there. "No fucking food," she muttered loudly. She dug her feet into her UGGs and picked up Colin with the blanket still around him like a burrito. "Come on," she said. They walked twenty minutes down Pipeline to McDonald's. His mother had forgotten her purse and the man said he couldn't give her the food. "Can he just eat? I'll come back later and pay, I promise. We had to walk here."

The man rolled his eyes and shoved the tray with the fries and burgers down the counter toward them. "Aight, ma'am. Do what you need to do."

At a table in the back, under a blaring TV, Colin ate and ate and ate but his mother didn't eat anything.

On the walk home, she put Colin on her back. Some cars were honking at them as they hiked up the shoulder of Pipeline Road. "Come on, let's take a rest." On the side of the road were some swampy woods. His mother pushed through tangles of foliage, pushed down tall grass with her knees, Colin still on her back. In the branches and weeds, there was so much trash: plastic bags, crushed beer cans, a dirty sock, a woman's tampon.

She was not stopping and not saying anything and then she said, "What if I left you out here." Colin's arms were choking her neck because he was sliding down her back. "What if I left you here, what would you do?" she asked again. He was silent. He gripped his legs around her harder. "Colin, I'm asking you a question. When someone asks you a question you better answer them. Otherwise you aren't going to get by. People are gonna think you're retarded or something." He pressed his wet mouth against the back of his mother's neck. "Colin!" she screamed. She wrangled his arms off her and he slid to the ground and caught his balance on his feet. "I'm asking you a question. You have to fucking answer me. Don't cry!"

"Bitch," he said and felt his whole body start trembling as the word flew out of his mouth. His mother stood back and bared her big yellow teeth. She looked straight over his shoulder at nothing, and just as it looked like she was going to pick him up, put him on her back again, and carry him all the way to their apartment, his mother slapped him in the face. "You don't get to call me that," she said. Colin slid to the ground, in a little ball, and then there was his mother, holding him there on the ground. He could still hear cars going down Pipeline. His mother's hair was in his mouth, her body pressing against him there in the dirt.

As they walked back to their apartment, she took his hand. "Colin." She said his name so quietly. "No one will ever love you like I do. You hear me?" She was almost whispering. "You might think love is out there, and you're gonna go searching for it one day, but then you will see that it's me who loves you more than anyone." The cars zoomed past. The sound of them was louder than his heartbeat and louder than his breathing. "I'm sorry," she muttered, holding her chin with the cup of her palm. "Colin, I'm sorry."

They were not going to renew the lease. They would be moving out of apartment 46 in a few weeks to live with Yolene for some time, all the way out in Hillsboro. "Will we go back to church?" Colin felt brave asking, thinking they could use a prayer. His mother didn't say anything. She was throwing their things into big cardboard boxes and black trash bags, taking thumbtacks out of the walls.

Right before move-out day, Colin and his mother sat on a bench at the Bell station waiting for the train. He had never taken a train, and his mother told him the night before that he would not be going to school the next day, that they would be taking a train and having an adventure. There was no one on the platform but a few nurses standing at the yellow line, blowing their cigarette smoke out over the empty rails. The station smelled like pee. Colin wished his mother had brushed her teeth and taken a shower, because he could smell her too. Earlier that morning, she had stood in front of the mirror and stared at herself: she was scooping out her zits, pinching the red mounds with her fingernails before scraping them clean of the little squirts of white ooze.

They had not eaten breakfast. His mother said they would get breakfast when they arrived. Colin was trying not to look up at her. She was making her eyes big and sad, and even though they were open all the way, it was as if she were staring backward into herself and not at the empty train tracks in front of them. There was nothing to look at but pigeons. He knew that pigeons were flying rats and they were everywhere. On the trash cans. Pecking at an open bag of Cheetos.

On the train, just as they sat down in seats attached to a blue table, the train started moving, ripping past a line of boxcars with bright, swirly graffiti. In one of them he saw a skinny man in nothing but his boxers rising up out of a foldout chair. He saw a few white ducks. He pressed his lips against the glass, power lines droopy with ivy smeared against the window.

In the seat next to him, his mother was leaning forward with her legs crossed, her knee bouncing up and down. Her hands were on her belly and she was in a stare, her eyes looking down at the floor while she bit off her fingernails and spit them out like chewed-up shells.

Colin was up on his knees, looking over his seat. He was staring at a sleeping man in a big coat. The man was wearing dirty socks with sandals. There was some kind of string hanging from the window, and Colin was wrapping it around his finger again and again, watching the man. "Don't stare. It's rude," his mother said, grabbing his neck. "Colin, sit down and look out the window. Don't waste the view. Look how pretty Texas is." There was nothing but fields of dead grass and sky, the squeaky, rattling sound of the train. Next to him was his mother, putting her necklace in her mouth and sucking on it.

They got off the train when the announcer said, "West Irving station." They didn't stop for food but continued walking down a gravel road. A big white truck started slowing down beside them: "Y'all need a ride?"

His mother looked down at Colin and looked back at the man, whose long, hairy arm hung out the window. "Thank you so much, sir, thank you. This is my son, Colin." She pushed him forward a little. They went around to the passenger side and climbed on in.

Inside the truck, the man had his heater on, and he was playing country music on the radio. "Y'all from around here?"

"Yes, sir," Colin heard his mother lie. "Our car broke down over on 35. My husband, he's out of town. But he'll be home tonight. We're gonna have a BBQ."

"That sounds nice. Don't tell me he's making you do all the cooking."

Colin sat between the man and his mother. Even though his mother was laughing and laughing, she was pressed against the door and Colin was pressed into her side. "Here we are. Just drop us off here is fine."

The neighborhood where they got out was a few scattered houses on several acres of land. Some of the houses had horses and pools in their backyards; Colin could see that even from the road. He knew whose neighborhood it was, but he wasn't going to say anything or ask anything. "Colin, maybe you should wait here," his mother said when they stopped by a tree. He did not want to wait under the tree, but his mother was already on the ground tying her shoes. She leaned forward to hug him and kiss him on the cheek but missed and kissed him on the mouth and Colin wiped the wetness off with his arm. "I'll be back, Colin. Please wait here." He sat down and zipped his jacket up over his head and nodded, then peeked up over the jacket and watched his mother take off through the tall yellow grass toward a big house.

Colin was sitting there in the grass, picking stickers out of his sweatpants. When his mother got to the door, he took off his glasses and let everything get blurry—the field and the horses and the house. He couldn't see her anymore, and he was thinking about what the preacher had said the day she knelt on the steps and all the people had gathered around her. That everyone there, without even knowing her, that they had loved her.

# THE TOUR

*by* CARMEN MARIA MACHADO

I WOULDN'T HAVE SEEN her if the baby hadn't cried across the platform, but the baby did, and I do. Past the beleaguered mother dandling the weeping infant and the dour teenager fussing with their phone, a tall, elegant smear of a woman is watching me from a train window. I recognize her, though I don't know where from. Her lips are parted slightly, like she's about to speak. She presses an open paperback to the glass; on the title page, a name and a phone number. Naomi.

I memorize the number with a mnemonic poem. The train takes a breath, begins to move. As soon as it is gone, I feel a wobbling beneath my feet, the sensation of stepping off a treadmill. By the time I emerge above the earth, I have Shifted; the poem remains.

I hate this part—the way I walk right afterward. I'm sure I look drunk or ill. I keep stopping and placing my palms against the sides of buildings, as if testing their sturdiness. I get to the venue, down a bottle of water, flip through the book I'm supposed to be talking about. I barely recognize myself. I went to Spain, learned Spanish.

Why? I look for all the usual suspects in the text, but this version of myself is coy—coyer than I knew possible. The copy on the back is helpful. It is about ambition, language, inheritance. It is about the dissolution of comfort zones. A critic calls it "brave." Fucking deadly.

"You're one of them, right?" a man in the audience asks. He has that face; a *This is more of a comment than a question* guy. They always look like him, like they walked in off the street because they saw someone else commanding an audience. "I read online that you were. If you are, isn't it slightly more appropriate to call this a work of fiction?"

"No," I say.

"But somewhere else, in some other... *place*... you would be saying yes, right?"

"I choose not to answer that question," I say, even though it is not really a question. In this timeline I seem to have developed a reputation for being a real diva anyway—prickly, unkind. Despite my unspeakable rudeness, I can feel the audience lean in closer. In that moment, I realize where I recognized the woman from: I'd swiped her away earlier that day, after checking out her profile for seven minutes. She'd been making the same face as she made in the train window, like she was about to open her mouth and speak. I sent her to the left because I couldn't bear to think what she would tell me.

They call it the Collapse, what happened with Solo 9. Ever since the comet appeared, scientists have been on the news doing their best to explain the unexplainable to a population who still can't grasp climate change. The scientists are not great. They describe the situation with a series of clumsy metaphors: a baseball going through a house of cards. A needle plunging through the weave of a heavy rope. A sweater snagging on an exposed nail. A bowling ball blowing through a crowd of pins. *Time-space continuum disruption personal worm-holes something something.* They handle the props awkwardly. We can measure it with machines, they promise. This is possible. That is probable. It could be. Maybe. They're the ones who started calling us "moles," which mixes the metaphor, but they think it's a better nickname than "worms." The pivot from the cliché exposes it; I have never hated an animal more.

One of the scientists, Dr. Joan Sooth, soon becomes famous; she declares things where the others hedge. People call her Auntie Joan because she is a woman and everyone wants their mother to have a beloved sister who understands what their mother does not. "The recent astronomical event has somehow modified the local physical laws here on Earth," Auntie Joan tells us in the weeks after Solo 9. "Every conscious choice results in a proliferation of near-identical universes. Normally they would be inaccessible to one another, but now, for some reason, for some people, they aren't. And for some of those people, they remain aware of where they've come from. They are continuous." Comedians sit across from her on the late-night shows, fiddling soberly with their prompt cards.

Most people don't feel their transitions. They're like babies being passed from person to person at a family reunion; startled for a split second, then adjusting almost immediately. No object permanence. But some of us remember. I do. Slip through timelines and know it. Constantly find themselves juggling slightly different versions of themselves. Everything in my suitcase will look half-familiar. I will feel vaguely sick. Occasionally I do throw up, though I've learned some tricks: tilting my head back, pressing my tongue to the roof of my mouth. I follow a ritual every time as a way to ground myself: I look for jewelry in my ears (if they're pierced), a watch on my wrist (if I have one), the color of my toenail polish (if I've bothered). It's like tapping your jeans for a wallet before leaving the house, but backward.

The problem with the Collapse—the problem with my collapse, specifically—was that right before it happened, I'd published another book. And not, for the first time in my life, a work of fiction. No. I'd been stupid enough to write nonfiction—even stupider, a memoir about a bad relationship. "Taking something back for myself," I assured my therapist. I'd been smug about finishing, pleased about preorders, ready to embark on a tour. I'd been in the air on my way to Minneapolis when Solo 9 blazed into the sky like an angel from Revelation. Everyone in the plane jostled one another to look out the windows. Their faces bubbled with light and color, as though we were around the same bonfire. Someone moaned softly, like they were seeing a lover's body for the first time. We are going to die, I thought.

But we didn't die. Or maybe somewhere we did, but here we didn't. The plane landed; an ashen bookseller picked me up from the airport. At my hotel I found myself struggling to look in the mirror; my vision felt soft, my body indistinct. I didn't realize what had happened until I was sitting in the stockroom, idly flipping through my own book. I frowned, bent closer. It was different. Little things—the place my ex and I went on vacation, the direction we walked through the streets of Brooklyn, the name of her ancient cat—but still. A misprint? Only, I was the misprint. I just didn't know it yet.

Fiction could have been fun. Or something. I can imagine it: touring through timelines to promote a novel instead. It is pleasant to imagine the permutations of a single fiction writer strained through many realities: the quirks of an ever-changing autobiography reflected in the characters' recollections. Fun, breezy conversations about craft and genre; the invention of characters as fragments of the author's self when the author's self is fragmented.

But no. With nonfiction, it is always a conversation about pain, about the ways I broke or the ways I let myself be broken. Even when it's a different book—even when the timeline I emerge into is free of *her*—it is about my cruelty, or someone else's cruelty, or my stupidity, or someone else's stupidity; our collective dysfunction, the ouroboros of suffering. In my original timeline it'd been such a weird book—analysis and confession; a particular flavor of betrayal—and even before it came out, I was tired of talking about trauma, the meticulous excavation and presentation of it. Everyone smiled gently and touched my arm and assured me I was articulate and brave, and no one ever simply said the truth: that I answered every question like an animal trying—and failing—to gnaw itself loose from a trap.

After the reading, I call Naomi from my hotel room. I'm not hoping for much. Here, her variant probably hadn't ridden the train earlier. Or mine hadn't. But maybe she'd be intrigued; maybe she'd want to meet up anyway. I have a whole speech prepared. She does not answer. I turn on the TV and hunt for her on Tinder, sending dozens of people into their own parallel timelines with every swipe. At the commercial break, I send her a text. She responds by calling.

"The woman from the subway," she says. "So good to hear your voice."

I am surprised—she has an accent. She also remembers me from somewhere else. No one has ever clocked me in that way. Another Shifter? I have never Shifted with anyone before—seen them in one timeline and then another, with their continuity binding us together. I feel a rush of adrenaline, endorphins, pleasure. I guess about the accent: Australian? "New Zealand," she says. "Australian is wider; the vowels open up. See?" And indeed her voice elongates and the vowels gape and I want to crawl inside.

"Close enough," I say.

"Not really," she says, the accent becoming clipped again. I am certain this is the end of the conversation but then she agrees to meet up the next time we're near each other.

"You're not in New York?" I ask.

"Sometimes, but not this time," she says.

The first time we cross over in the same city (T88), we have dinner at a very fancy and expensive restaurant in the West Village, where the schtick is that the waiters take your order, bring you food, and charge you at the end of the meal. She sits across from me, letting her knees touch mine. The first time she does it, I bite the tines of my fork; my skull rings like a bell.

"What do you do? For a living, I mean?"

"Consulting," she says. She does not elaborate.

"And you Shift?"

"Yeah."

"Which timeline are you in?"

"What do you mean? This one."

"I mean, what number are you on? You know, what's your count?"

"I don't count them," she says.

I am eating a cornichon and inhale a breath of vinegar. I cough. "You don't *count* them?"

"You do? Doesn't that make you feel tired?"

I am tired. Too tired to be teased. Nearby, a table of many-worlds truthers are arguing that slippage isn't real; moles are liars; it's all a conspiracy. I look at Naomi and roll my eyes, but she seems lost in thought, as though seriously considering the argument. Then she turns to me; runs her fingers in lazy lemniscates on the underside of my wrist.

"I don't want anything serious," she says. "I really don't. I'd prefer to enjoy you."

"I would like to be enjoyed," I say, my throat dry. I have been single for two years; every timeline is similarly lonely. I have been taking so many medications for the side effects of the Shifting that I haven't come in an eon. An orgasm feels less like a thing my body can do and more like an ancient prophecy that has wound its way through ten generations of elders.

"I'm very good at it," she says.

"I believe you," I tell her.

"What would you like?" she asks.

"I would like to be gone."

She pays the bill, and I can already imagine it, as if it's already happened: the two of us against my front door, her hand down the front of my jeans. But then she smiles—wry, amused. "We're about to Shift," she says. "Can you feel it?"

I can. I nod.

"See you soon," she says.

In the new timeline—T89—I am walking down the street stunned with want, swollen and soaked as August. My jeans chafe my thighs raw. And then suddenly I am in a hotel room in Phoenix (T90), alone, with an episode of *Law & Order: SVU* playing on mute. That night, I dream of my original timeline, the one I left behind. How imperfect it was. How no self who will ever occupy it will understand it as intimately as I do.

Naomi looks me up in each new timeline; I get emails, texts. She is in Cape Town; she is in Amsterdam; she is in Cairo; she is in South Dakota. Once, I receive a physical letter with a phone number, and when I call, a stranger tells me she's at a convent (a convent!) in France (in France!). I am looking at plane tickets when I Shift again, and three days later we are drinking wine in a tiny bookshop in Crown Heights. I tell her about how I almost visited the convent, to find her. She laughs.

"I bet you were there seducing all the nuns," I say.

"Just the one," she says. "But I was actually devout. It was—"

"Hot?"

"Holy. But also hot. Did you know that in some traditions archangels cannot help but stand before God?"

"Because he's God?"

"Because they have no knees."

She pulls up the Bible on her phone, shows me. Then, "Are you queer in all of yours?"

"Yeah. You?"

"Usually. Once, I was married to a man, but I was clearly closeted. We overlapped for three weeks and he had all these *feelings* I couldn't care less about and I said, 'Who's the lesbian, you or me?' and he got very quiet as he put all the pieces together."

"That sounds hard."

"At least I didn't have to witness the aftermath. I think he would have sued me for full custody of the kids. I mean, I think he did. I just didn't have to be around to see it. Some other version of me got to bear that burden. Whatever. Who cares."

There is something huge moving against my lips; a goldfish of a confession. How much I worry about my other selves, the ones that get left behind. I'd like to imagine they're all as messed up as me, but it is entirely possible that any number of them are far more well-adjusted, concerned with their sense of selves and the meaning of existence within the framework of their impossible situation, instead of treating their slippage as an endless vacation. I especially wonder about the ones who avoided the Big Bad Wolf. Maybe they are more interesting, less needy. Maybe they're the ones Naomi could be serious about.

"God, I hate this conversation," she says. "I hate that every gay date eventually includes a coming-out story or a rape story or both."

"We don't have to talk about anything," I say.

"Or an abuse story," she continues. "Jesus."

"In fact," I say, "I'd rather not."

We go to a karaoke bar and she sings Patsy Cline and she is so beautiful up there on the stage that I am kind of scared and my jaw hurts. When she gets down, I hand her a drink and say, "It's nice, seeing you. Isn't this nice? It's nice how we can see each other when we happen to be in the same timeline. It has been so lonely."

She clutches my face in her hands, leans so close I discover that her eyes are not, fully, brown. "That's not very brave of you," she says. This pronouncement goes to my molten core. She is right. I am not brave. I am a coward of the highest order. She runs a thumb over my lip.

"Do you know what your face says?" she asks. I shake my head. She puts one phrase in my right ear, one in my left. *Hurt me,* she says, then, *"don't hurt me."*

Hurt me, don't hurt me. Tattoo it on my collarbone, I think, or else I'm going to forget.

I would call my mother for advice, but our relationship is almost never good, no matter what timeline I'm in. Sometimes we're estranged; sometimes I can't locate her. Once, she was dead. Or is dead. She's dead somewhere, still. If I ever get hold of her, I know what she'll say. She'll say, *Isn't it funny how they call them daughter universes? All of those daughters. Endless, useless, ungrateful. Lucky enough to have choices; too selfish to appreciate them.*

Naomi calls me from Minneapolis, tells me she's touching herself. "I'm outside at a farmers market," I tell her, "but you go right ahead." The landscape of her breath is dotted with idle conversation. I shop, ask my questions, perform my business. "Do you have any

blood oranges? Do you take credit cards? What about oyster mush-
rooms? I'll take that basket. Beefsteak tomatoes? I have my own bag.
Chokecherries? Thank you, thank you, thank you."

"You know," she says into my ear when I am thanking a hobbled
vendor who is, conservatively, ninety-seven years old, "I am going
to fuck you until you can't stand up." I can smell her through the
produce: vegetal and garish. She comes as I am sitting near the edge
of a fountain, eating a peach.

In T93, we go to a zoo, to the small mammal house, and she
points out the star-nosed mole, with his extra thumb and a face like
Cthulhu's. The nose is an Eimer's organ, exquisitely sensitive, she
says, while tracing a pattern on my palm. "Sure," I say. "*Fuck*. Okay."
She tells me about a prophetic text from the fourteenth century called
the Prophecy of Merlin, which declared that the sixth king of England
after King John would be a mole, a proud and contemptible and cowardly person with skin like a goat. She breaks down the etymology of
the world *mole*. She takes me back to her apartment and kisses me so
slowly I want to scream. She wants to take me to a beach, show me
off, she says, as her hot breath punctuates my collarbone, my thighs,
my feet. She wants me to meet her friends—some of them, anyway.
She wants to take me to a hotel, to make me homemade noodles, to
show me her favorite heist movie. She wants to do everything to me
and know everything about me, and it's not clear where doing ends
and knowing begins.

So I tell her. I tell her about my ex-girlfriends and my auto-
immune disorder; how I've been on tour with my new, stupid book
for an eternity and an age. I tell her that my books keep selling and
selling. In every timeline. I keep waiting to wake up in a world where
the book never sold, or I never wrote it, or no one has heard of me.

"I think," she says, "that's what it means to be canonized. To be
being canonized. How does it feel?"

Startled, I Shift. T99. I am running somewhere, though I don't know where, or from someone, though I don't know who. The details curl into my mind like tendrils of smoke, but I ignore them. The streets are rouged with dusk.

In some realities, I have a friend named Rebecca. She is often, though not always, a poet. Her mind is the same every time, though: acidity rendered into tenderness. She is not a mole herself, but she believes me each time I say, "We're friends," is comfortable with the fact that I've sought her out even in the timelines where she doesn't know me. In this one, though, she remembers me—we met in Girl Scouts in seventh grade. I describe Naomi to Rebecca, and she thoughtfully lobs a chunk of bread into a pond.

"She sounds like a fuckboy," she says.

"No," I say. "No. I'd know."

"Like a quantum fuckboy."

"Ugh. Maybe."

"It's like basic physics. Or base physics."

I watch the ducks rush in from all angles. They are ravenous.

"Fucking a fuckboy is great," she says. "It's hot. But that doesn't mean it's a good idea."

In one timeline, I open to a random page of my own book and read a sentence I've never read before: "Does the earth not have veins of ore; do rivers not have mouths?" I imagine the self that wrote this sentence. She dated someone in her twenties who really liked hiking. They got into the habit of fucking in the woods. She had this thought one afternoon when she was staring at the tree limbs above her head, listening to her girlfriend drink her.

In another, I find myself talking about some version of the book I thought I remembered—the wily, frenetic take on an abusive relationship, the first one, the only one I remember writing—and only when I step off the stage to sign the books of bewildered patrons do I realize that in this timeline it's a memoir-cum-craft book: *Terror as Dialectic*, whatever that means. I stare at the bio. This bitch got a PhD, I realize in horror—real horror. *I* got a PhD.

In another timeline, I go to my dead mother's house. Her death is so recent that all her possessions are there, still in the fading light. I stand in her closet and it feels like being in the unearthed tomb of a mad and minor pharaoh. Instead of Canopic jars, there are handbags, high heels you could drink out of. I lean into the clothes to smell them, to get some sense of my own loss. Her perfume still lingers, though behind it there is some other scent. Sweet. Almost yeasty. Our estrangement? Could such a thing have a smell? In the very back of the closet, I find several boxes of my books. Downstairs, there is a flyer pinned to the fridge beneath a VEGAS magnet. Dr. Joan Sooth happens to be lecturing at a local college this evening. I go in my dead mother's stead. During the Q&A, I ask her about Naomi, though not by name. "What does it mean," I ask, "if two moles keep Shifting together, into the same timelines?"

She thinks, then responds: "It almost never happens," she says. "And if it were to happen once, it certainly wouldn't happen *again*. You're talking about a quantum entanglement of a very strong bond."

"Destiny?" I ask.

She shakes her head and says something about particle spin and superposition. Then she stabs a pencil through a folded-up piece of paper. "See?" she says. "Like this." Around me, people are nodding. They have no idea, like me. They are such liars.

The next time, Naomi and I meet at a restaurant but don't make it past the appetizers. Outside, she asks me to grab her hair, which I do. Her head feels sturdy, distinctly alive.

"I want to come somewhere where someone can hear me," she says.

"Don't you mean 'go'?" I ask.

"I want to go somewhere where someone can hear me come and come somewhere where someone can hear me go."

We go to a hotel. She strips me, inhales. She spits into my mouth, runs her thumb over my lips. She does it again. She tells me to swallow. When I do, I feel her body jolt like it's been electrified. "Good girl," she says. "Good fucking girl."


In T103, when I leave the cultural center, I run into a beautiful twinkish couple who are, clearly, waiting for me. The one on the right has an enamel pin on their lapel that features an image of Solo 9. The other has earrings that say bitch boy. They wanted to say hello, but they didn't want to take up time in my signing line, they explain. "We're moles," one of them says. "Both of us." Only then do I notice the wedding rings. I am so surprised, I sit down right there on the curb. I can feel the cold pavement through my tights. They sit on either side of me, like acolytes. They tell me their names and I immediately forget them.

"You're married," I say. It is all I can say.

"We kept running into each other in various timelines," says Bitch Boy, "so we decided to give it a shot."

"Who else could you build a life with?" says Lapel Pin. "Who else would share all the same memories, the same histories?"

"Sometimes we Shift and we're apart from each other, but then we just find each other again."

"We always go to a shop, buy rings, drink champagne."

"It sounds wild, but it works."

They take me out to drinks, and a few sips into my beer I fall asleep on Bitch Boy's shoulder. They take me home and lay me out on their couch and cover me in an afghan. I Shift in the night, and wake up staring into the smooshed, dignified face of an Angora. A beautiful woman I don't recognize comes into the bedroom with a cup of coffee.

"Hey," she says. I stare at her. She pulls back a little. The cat butts my chin with her head and purrs.

"Oh," she says. "Oh. You—did you—?"

I feel a little scrap of the memory bloom—her unfolded on the bed, wet and pink as a baby bird. She lets me drink the coffee, but I leave soon afterward. I cannot bear to be a stranger twice.

Once—and only once—I step out of a café in Bed-Stuy and I am on top of a mountain. The transition is so violent that I lie down in the grass, shivering and waiting for the nausea to pass. When I stand up, I see Naomi sitting loose-limbed on a log, the entirety of the Catskills staged behind her like a commercial. She is sharpening a stick with a pocketknife; the light from the sunset is caught in her curls. She looks up from her task and her smile makes me dizzy. We are here, we are alone. I know that we have been on this trip for days. I know that if I were to open my phone, it would be a perfect mélange of sexually explicit photos and domestic requests: picking up coffee or bringing home takeout. I know that every scent on her will be intensified. I know that if I were to pull her into the dirt and kiss her, every crease would taste smoky and sour and unwashed. The me in this timeline was worth the drive into this wilderness. I smile.

She is building a carapace of kindling over logs. She is striking a match in the civil twilight.

Then I am nowhere, then I am sitting in a greenroom across from a platter of cold cuts. There is a single bite out of a rolled-up bit of salami. The side, not the end. A chaotic bite. Mine? Someone else's? A prop meant to illustrate the Collapse's effect on wormholes? A bad metaphor, regardless.

I look around for Naomi, even though I know she's not there. I stand and puke into a tiny trash can next to the dressing table.

A publicist comes in, holds my hair back.

"Thank you," I say to her. "Sorry."

"That was a doozy, huh," she says. "Is the salami bad?"

"I think I may have come out of a dead timeline," I tell her. When I straighten, she is looking sad and a little frightened.

"'Dead timeline' is a misnomer," I say to her. "I was dead, I mean—not the timeline itself."

Her smile is strained.

"I'm sure you were there," I say. "I'm sure you were fine."

As I wait to go onstage, I wonder how I died. I run through all my worst nightmares: a train derailment. Plane crash. Choking on a grape while alone in my hotel room. Shoved onto the subway tracks. I settle on the least upsetting: an aneurysm blooming in postcoital sleep.

The talk show host laughs when I come onstage. We're friends, I guess. The audience goes wild.

When we are done, Dr. Joan Sooth comes out for her weekly segment. She looks polished but less severe than the circumstances warrant. She is very charming. Afterward, in the greenroom, I ask her for some advice.

She listens thoughtfully, her pen moving over a Post-it. When I'm done, she hands the note to an assistant—a lunch order, I realize. "It's a strange coincidence," she says. "But exactly that—a coincidence. It's random. It denotes nothing at all."

\* \* \*

In T107, I ask Naomi if this means something. The way we hunt for each other in each new timeline. "How did you feel, on the mountain?" I ask.

"I think," she says, "you are making a—"

"Don't say it."

"—*something* out of a molehill."

I take a deep breath. I am relaxed. I am a free spirit. "I suppose you're right." I eat a shrimp.

"You're not being honest with me," she says.

"What do you mean?"

"You keep pretending like you're chill but you're not chill."

I open my mouth to insist otherwise but the lie dies on my lips.

"You want to control the situation," she says. "You're not letting yourself enjoy it. I need you to be in the moment."

"I can't be in the moment—I can't be in any moment, that's the point." The vacation has ended. The labor of existing has restarted.

I tell her about the couple, the one I met. The way they affirm their feelings over and over again, against impossible odds.

"I think we should take a break. Take some timelines off. This is getting to be way too much, too quickly." She looks down at her chipping manicure. "Maybe we should go ahead and end it now."

"I don't want this to be over."

"Somewhere, it already is. Or it never began. Do you understand that? One day we are going to exhaust our shared timelines, move past each other."

I am annoyed because I know. Of course I know. I tuck my head between my knees. "I feel like you're calling all the shots," I say, "and it freaks me out." The person who cares less always calls the shots. It is a position of strength.

"I need you to be honest with me," she says. "Why is this so important to you?"

I have no response.

"If you don't want to be honest with me, that's your choice," she continues.

I open my mouth to contradict her but I am suddenly in the dark, somewhere quite warm. A mosquito whines over my head. I was beginning to sympathize with the truthers. Maybe the many worlds were a lie. Or maybe the lie was that any of the many worlds would be different. Every one I went to, I found the same shit.

We reconnect two days and eight timelines later. I am so dizzy I can drink only ginger ale.

"I am ready to be honest," I say.

"Oh?" she says. "Tell me."

"I like you. I like you a lot. I'm not saying I'm in love with you, but I want to keep seeing you. I don't understand why you want to make this stop. Doesn't the chemistry—I mean, don't you—?"

"I don't want it that badly," she says. The sentence falls between us like a blob of bird shit. She tries again. "I would like to be friends regardless," she suggests. "I'm not asking it of you. It's merely a statement of fact."

"That makes me feel terrible," I say.

"*That* makes me uncomfortable," she says. Her sweetness has evaporated.

"You asked me," I say. "You asked me to be honest."

"Well," she says, her voice dry. "That was brave of you, I suppose."

"There is a word in Arabic, *ebky*," I say. "It means 'to ask someone to cry.'"

She is silent.

"It's unfair, whether you say it in English or in Arabic," I clarify.

We part ways. A little while later, she texts me, suggests that if

I'm not in therapy already, it might suit me. I think about this—endless first sessions with a sequence of mental health professionals, each more useless than the last. I am so cool, I send her a photo of myself in a bra. There is a brief silence, then she writes, "More." I send her another one, bra off. An hour goes by, then two. Eventually, she writes, "I can't do this right now."

When I tell this story to Rebecca, three days and two timelines later (T127), I remind her that she called Naomi a fuckboy.

"That sounds about right," she says. She is a mother here; as she talks, she keeps an eye on her toddler, who is dropping dirt down her pants. "I was actually gonna say that now. Fucking a fuckboy is great. It's hot. But that doesn't mean it's a good idea."

"You already said that," I say. The toddler turns and shows us the universes she has made with the dark smudges of her hands.

"I was right then, and I'm right now."

Then I am standing next to a river, then sobbing in an alley, and then I wake up because I've been asleep.


In T139, I have written a book of well-received essays that includes one about the Moberly-Jourdain incident of 1901. Two women go for a walk and become convinced that they have slipped through time to the court of Louis XVI, in the eighteenth century. It is a time-slip, not a timeline-slip, but I feel strongly connected to them just the same. Theories include the obvious—the high-strung women encountered a costume party and jumped to the most ludicrous possible conclusion—but I prefer the one where they had a lesbian folie à deux, a shared bubble of madness that stemmed from their unarticulated and unconsummated desire for each other.

"Why this incident?" a woman asks. I've seen her before, in other timelines. She must be a fan. I wonder whether she'd be horrified if

I told her, or embarrassed. *I see you*, I could tell her. I won't, though. I wouldn't wish this kind of exposure on anyone.

I have such a good answer. "Dykes have no respect for natural law," I quip. Slippage is gay. Time travel is queer. I say something about timelines and scissoring and string theory. Schrödinger's pussy. Spooky strap-ons at a distance. Everyone laughs, because I am funny, because I am very good at what I do.

Back in the hotel, a news story informs me that scientists are worried about the moles. Psychological instability. Rare cancers. Unusual perspectives. A pattern of dissociation, mania, depression.

Naomi calls me. She's in the Netherlands. She's high. "I've been thinking about being inside you," she says, "and that's bad."

I ride the jolt of this news from the thrill of the opening to its bitter end. "Why," I ask, "is that bad?"

"I want you too much. It puts things in jeopardy. It makes uncomplicated things complicated."

When she hangs up, I climb into the bed in all my clothes. What a problem, I think. To be liked too much. What a problem to have.

The crowd at the reading in T217 is massive. I don't think I've ever had a crowd that big—for any book, in any timeline. People fill the chairs and squeeze into corners; others sit sprawled against a wall. I squint at a poster on an easel; the title tells me nothing. So I begin to catalog the other books I can remember. The memoir about my ex but with a single word altered; the same, but with every sentence exactly as I wrote it, untouched. The version where she died in a car accident and I mourned her without ever having understood what she was. The version where we got married. The version where she was hit by lightning on our honeymoon and I couldn't get the smell of burning out of my head. The version where we had a child who loved her so, so much—and me, not as much. But other books too: The memoir of erotic discovery. The tell-all about my youth pastor. The book-length critical defense of the amorality of the creation of fiction. The Oulipian reimagining of key events of my youth. The slender lyrical essay about my mother. The annotated autobiography where I tell a sober story about family narratives and howl in grief in the footnotes. The book-length meditation on gender. The self-deprecating essay collection. Uncountable others. Infinite others. Mine, all.

I read from a page at random. It is a horny book, even for me. The Q&A begins.

"Can you," asks a feathery woman in a caftan, "tell us why you have chosen to write about sex? To objectify women, even as a woman yourself. There is something about the focus on sex here that feels— ugly. Anti-feminist. Pornographic, almost."

The audience visibly tenses. I can feel, in some distant wisp of newly acquired memory, that a variation on this question had previously sent me into a public frenzy on the West Coast, and that the incident was somewhat notorious, and that it is shocking that someone has asked me this question again. I tilt the microphone toward my face like I'm going to take a bite.

"Desire," I say, "is not our greatest problem. Getting fucked is easy. It's choosing. Every decision you make whittles away at your future; that is the contradiction of choice. Don't you understand what I'm afraid of? It's exactly what you should be afraid of, but worse. Every time you flip on a light switch or kiss someone or take a different route, you're snipping away a thread from yourself and birthing infinite selves. You become the mother of many timelines and kill a little bit of yourself at the same time. In the end, some people are afraid to choose love. If you're going to slaughter a little piece of yourself, it might as well be for love, right?

"I am an artist, yes, but I'm also a horny, lonely, overeducated idiot. I don't want to be on a tour. I don't enjoy meeting new people. I don't want to talk or laugh or explain. I don't want to sign books or sell them or read from them. I just want to get fucked. Do you understand? Every time I wake up in some new timeline, I'm not thinking about the kaleidoscopic variations of human observation and the multiplicity of permutations of human choice-making that led to the exact moment that I am experiencing; all I'm thinking about is getting fucked. I'm standing in the gorgeous, hallowed, specific intersection of my own design, something holy and rarefied, and all I'm thinking is, You dumb slut, you dumb, wet slut, all you want is someone to obliterate you, to cut you down where you stand, to *fuck you to death*, what is *wrong* with you? You piece of shit, you cunt-struck lunatic, what the fuck are you thinking except *nothing*, you are thinking about *nothing*, you have no knees and you can only stand or fall. And at night you lie there thinking, *Love me, love me, love me, love me, love me, love me, love me, love me, love me, love me, love me, love me, love me, love me, love me, love me, love me, love me, love me, love me, love me, love me, love me, love me, love me, love me, love me, love me, love me, love me, love me, love me, love me, love me, love me, love me, love me, love me, love me, love me, love me, love me, love me, love me, love me, please love me, love me, love me, love me, love me, love me, love me, love me, love me, love me, love me, love me, love me, love me, love me, love me, love me, love me, love me, love me, love me, love me, love me, love me, love me, love me, love me, love me—*"

The host wrestles the microphone from my grasp so efficiently, so deftly, I know that she learned the technique in a self-defense class. In that reality, I am at the beginning of a very minor but very real nervous breakdown. But the next morning, I wake up in a different city, and this time I've written a voicey travel memoir, and the bookstore owner has sent me an apologetic email about the previous night's event. "I'm sorry we had so few bodies in the seats," she tells me. "Next time."

\*　\*　\*

I like a photo of Naomi holding a baby possum at a wildlife rescue center, and she DMs me. She is married in this timeline, she says, but she does not care. She tells me what she wants me to do to her. She tells me where, which restaurant, which table, which drink I should order, how slow and deliberate, how hard and fast. She tells me who is watching, how many of them, how many of them are men, how long she'll watch me, what she wants me to do while she's watching me, what she wants the men to do. Where the mirrors are. It moves from sexy to sexily implausible to illegal to physically impossible, and I am so turned on that when she is done I talk my way into an employee bathroom at an Au Bon Pain and masturbate silently against the wall.

Two days later, we meet at a bowling alley and she asks me to give her compliments.

"What kind of compliments?" I whip the ball; it rolls across the gutter and launches into a neighboring lane.

"You know, compliments. I want to feel good."

And so I do. It's a hard line to walk; if I project, she'll sense it; if I misidentify a trait, she'll pull away. I must be honest, accurate, flattering. I tell her how I love the way she unwinds her curls when she's thinking; the provocative bell-shape of her mouth; the way her voice sounds like a clarinet's middle note stooping beneath a doorframe. I tell her she is canny, funny, hot. I recite the poem I used to memorize her number. "Mmm," she says. She becomes quiet, guarded. I can tell that telling her about the poem has made her uncomfortable; I fear that was not the tone of compliment she was seeking.

"That's sweet," she says. "I'm so glad we get to be friends." I twitch a little; my body's betrayal. "Just friends," she says.

I tell her that I can't be "just friends" with someone who has looked at—no, no, no—*seen* my asshole. I hate that I am opening myself up to someone who is closing up in front of me. My mother once told me, when I was young, to protect my heart, and I have never learned, not once. I can't even protect my asshole.

"I think the next time will be the last time," she says, like she's made her choice from a long and complicated menu. I feel faint, and sit down, and when I open my eyes, the bowling alley is an endless ocean and I am bent over the side of a fine boat and the water keeps moving up to meet me.

I meet Rebecca at a rage room. In this timeline, we had been coworkers as twentysomethings, working shoulder to shoulder at a miserable nonprofit until we quit within a week of each other, and we have coffee once a month to stay in touch. Here, today, now, we take sledgehammers to a television set.

"You know," she says, "when you broke up with your bad ex, you kept saying, 'Maybe the problem is we met each other at the wrong time?' You kept positing that if you'd met when you were older or younger or whatever, you might have been kinder to each other. What if, with some people, there is no right time? What if there's no right timeline? What if some people will always remain inaccessible to you?" She picks up a vase and lobs it into the wall. Punishment.

I crush a sequence of ceramic figurines in my hands. Crow. Dinosaur. A teddy bear in a ruff. "Even—?"

"*Even* if your bodies fit together beautifully. Some people can't help but be drawn to the impossible. The impossible is hot."

When we leave the rage room, our phones ping with a news alert. "Dr. Joan Sooth, dead in a car accident at age 67." She will be alive soon, I think, even as I bend in half while Rebecca rubs circles on my back. Most of the time, she will be alive soon.

On our last tour stop—seven timelines later—Naomi takes me out on the town. Really takes me out. We go to one bar and suck down tequila shots, licking salt off our hands. She runs her hands up my dress, kisses me so hard in a booth that we scare away a waitress. In a hotel room, we have sex until we can't stand up—her promise, delivered—and the next day she takes me to an art museum. I can feel her gaze on me the entire time, like a leash I don't want to take off. We go back to the hotel. We try to go to dinner but we never get there; she holds me down and puts her hand inside me and wraps another hand around my throat and it is like she's closing a circuit. She is deliberate, cruel, so agonizingly slow. She is never going to look for me again, I realize. I can feel it, then: the beginning of an orgasm, gathering behind my tailbone.

"Why are you crying?" she asks into my ear. She does not break her rhythm.

"Because I'm going to come," I tell her. "And I don't want to."

"Why not?"

"Because when I come, this will all be over," I say. "I miss you already."

"It will be over, yes," she says. Her voice is so soft and teasing. I sob and swallow a mouthful of air. "It will be over. But wasn't it so good?"

I cannot answer. Language has dissolved in me. I cannot bring it back any more than I can unmix saltwater.

"You have to come," she says. "I want you to."

"Please," I say. Please what? Please don't go. Please don't stop.

She shakes her head. Inside of me, something unfurls; a bat waking into dusk.

"Come here," she says. Then she says it again, and I feel my brain parsing it along two distinct axes. Come, here. Come here. Here would be a place to Shift, I think. To start all over again.

The next timeline doesn't come, but I do. I come the way you drag a child in her Sunday clothes through the gravel of the church parking lot. I come with a reluctant spread, somewhere between bottoming and bottoming out. I feel like a needle plunging through a weave of heavy rope. I feel like a baseball going through a house of cards. I ascend in elevation; I fall back to earth. The sound I make is half moan, half wail. I am still shaking, whimpering, when she kisses me goodbye.

"It would have been romantic, you and me," she says into my ear. It is so breathtakingly mean, I have no response.

Far beneath us, a subway train rumbles through a tunnel. The sound travels up and up and breaks around me. Then I am nowhere; then I am on a stage in a room full of people who are all staring at me, their hands on my book and my book on their laps. Rebecca is there, her face gentle with attention. My ex, expressionless. Dr. Joan Sooth, with a woman—my mother?—speaking into her ear. The book in front of me has a close-up detail from *The Garden of Earthly Delights* and the title—*Shifters*—in a clean and modern font. When I open it, I see Naomi's name over and over. A bold choice. Legally risky, ethically fraught. A terrible idea. I flip to the end. We don't make it either. Maybe none of us do.

I turn back to chapter 1. I meet the audience's eyes over the microphone; they are watching and waiting and all I can do—today, tomorrow, always, again—is tell them what I know. "I wouldn't have seen her," I read, "if the baby hadn't cried."

# CELESTIAL CITY

*by* LISA KO

IF THERE IS A god, he looks like Eletha W. surveying 644th Street on a Saturday morning with her hair to her ankles and her bosom quivering inside her shirtdress. Yan insists that god is real, and every day she prays like it will deliver us from 644th Street and into the miracle of the Central Forest. Inside me grows an asphalt tree, waiting.

Eletha W. lives in a cellar apartment across the street and does not appreciate disrespect. She is missing one front tooth and likes to wrinkle her nose when she talks, and her armpits smell like wet cheese. One day, when I was playing jacks in the alley with the younger girls, I saw Eletha on the stoop in her petticoat, god right there. I let the ball bounce out of my hand and roll into the gutter and into oblivion. At home, Mama swatted my butt cheeks with a pickle board.

Oblivion is where the lost things go and they are never found. Things I have lost: my little brother Ng; the twins born in the summer of my second year, whose faces I never saw; one sock from a pair that was supposed to last me throughout my eleventh year; one father, who left one evening in the autumn of my fourteenth year and has yet to be seen even six weeks later.

Yan says Eletha W. is a zafty strumpet but Yan has nothing but shame and regret, even if the worst thing she has ever done was to steal a bit of her brother's slice of salt pie. When her mother caught her, Yan spent eleven hours in constant prayer, lying facedown on the buckled floor in her family's apartment, above ours, refusing to respond when I called her name. Yan is skinny all over, even skinnier than me, with brown skin that freckles and thick bangs that hang down into the tops of her eyes.

Yan's brother said Baba was slaughtered dead in Bottle Alley. I yanked his earlobe and told him I hoped he would get slaughtered too. Yan told us both we were going to hell. Later, she apologized to me.


On a warm night near the harvest moon, eight weeks after we last saw Baba, I follow Eletha W. as she tucks away from 644th Street. Mama hangs pin socks from the rope in the courtyard, humming a ditty. I wish there was a song she would sing about me, a song where I am a girl with eyes like stars, like Eletha's. But Mama sings only about birds and trees.

I creep down the sidewalk after Eletha's skirts. She clops furiously through the streets, a steam liner, the moon upstairs a sickly yellow. On the corner of Ash and 630th a horse carriage is waiting, the horse sleek and black, stomping its hooves on the cobblestones. The carriage is round and sparkling, a lost jewel uptown. Women stare as the little door opens and Eletha hitches her skirt and climbs up, exposing her cloth boots, her feet the size of roast fowl. When the skirts fall back, her feet disappear. I stand in the gaslight. Zafty, one woman croaks. Hussy, another hisses. Eletha disappears into the cavern of the jewel. Her face is calm, a small ruffle on the high collar brushing her heavy jaw, her dark hair coiled, with the front puffy and high. She shuts the door and the carriage rattles away.

The next night and the next I hang the wash for Mama. I squeeze the gray water from strangers' bloomers and petticoats. I rub frayed bedclothes and sheeting until my fingers are sore and red. Lye burns. Mama sings about a songbird twirling through pink blossoms and grass and I whip the sodden bloomers against the washboard, spraying the walls with bubbles and dirt. The sound of the heavy cloth thumping against metal is so pleasing that I do it again. Whip. Hit. I am a daughter. Whip. Hit. Baba is gone. When Mama sees the mess, she holds the iron rod to my face, so close I can see the heat steaming, and threatens to sear me. I ask forgiveness. I am sorry for Ng. I am sorry for the twins. I am sorry for Baba and all the nights I dream of suckling Eletha W.'s bosom. If I were Yan, I'd pray. But I am not Yan, only another small girl in a yellowing shirtdress. My ass stays as bony and flat as Yan's forehead on the floor when she is in deep and utmost regret.

My little brother Ng was born in the winter, after the New Year. It was the wettest winter even in the memories of adults. Damp woolens, frozen toes, the skin on our hands purple and shriveled. Cold seeping up through the air shaft.

The twins I cannot remember; I know only that they were alive and then they were dead, like a flower Mama told me about that bloomed once in the morning and wilted by evening. Shriveled-flower twins. Were they boys or girls? I asked Mama. Boy, girl, she said. One of each, she said. They did not have names.

Ng lived for two years. I bounced him. I removed his deposits from the chamber bucket and poured them down the air shaft. He clung to me like soot to oily skin. When he held my hand it was like fresh sunshine. He knew words: my name, Yan's name, *Mama, Baba, ball, eat, milk, sleep*. During the wettest winter he turned to nothing, with arms reduced to shrunken twigs. Black-prune eyeballs. Blue-purple cheeks. Mama sent me to Yan's, sent for a visiting nurse, who could not save him. Yan's mother fed us turnip cake and tea. Do not drink gutter water, our mothers told us, but babies did not know better. Babies could not understand. Did I not know better? Under whose watch had Ng pressed his hands into the leaking wet stream running through the rear courtyard, then pressed his hands to his face, clapping droplets into his mouth and nose, his baby pudge? Had it been me? When I came home from Yan's three days later, he was gone.

The harvest moon passes and then winter is almost here and Baba still has not come home. I ask Mama where he is and she says he is working.

Where? I ask.

He is on a ship. He set off on a trip.

I'm not sure if I believe her. She keeps looking away, and her fingers dance over one another. Her hair is wavy and gray.

What kind of ship? I ask.

It makes—iron.

I blink at her. Where is the ship going?

East, she says, waving her hand in the air in some vague direction. To the ocean.

Baba did many kinds of jobs. Ferrying rocks to build new buildings, stoking a fire that powered a factory. He picked garbage in the Central Forest, helped Mama in the laundry. He did work on the docks. Filthy, dangerous work, Mama said. Boat work, he said. But there was work and there was money and he went to the water.

On a night where there is no moon I follow Eletha again. Mama is asleep in her chair with her mouth open. This time, Eletha walks to the Boulevard to take the El. I have prepped. Laundry washed and hung, mounds of shirtwaists. I steal pennies from Mama's sack and clutch them in my palm.

The El squeals around the curve past windows where children sit, staring, and mothers string shirts onto the lines in rear courtyards like our rear courtyard; throughout the city there are rear courtyards within rear courtyards and in some cases, I imagine, smaller rear courtyards tucked into those, and on and on, full of families like our family but not like our family at all. They have orange hair. They have straw noses.

Downtown, Eletha gets off at Fifth Avenue and I follow her to the street where the buildings rise higher and everywhere there are trolleys clanging. Fine women in gloves and fancy clothes side-eye Eletha and shove her gently. She stumbles, nearly skimming the gutter. I want to knuckle the fine women in the face. I want to tip their high hats into slop.

We swing through clusters of men. Up ahead are lights, the nickelodeon, the vaudeville, the hurdy-gurdy, light bulbs for letters. Signs for shirtwaists and hash loaf, pork chops five ways. Oysters. I have never eaten them. I picture them slip-sliding down Eletha's soft gullet. Outside stand so many men. I look for Baba's face but none of them resemble Baba.

Little girl, whispers a man in a black suit. I dodge his hands. Two men without suit jackets leer over me. Coming to the show? They laugh, sharp. I push them—Eletha! She approaches a wide black door and the men part. I run to the door but a man blocks me, his arm at my forehead. Another man takes me by the neck. Who are you with? You can't go in there.

My friend, I say, but he pushes me back. His face is red and wrinkled beneath his thick brown beard, spittle whitening at the corners of his mouth.

The end of time is a place I like to go. At the end of time Baba sits with his shoes off and moistens his tobacco pipe with soft flicks of his tongue. He rocks—front, back; front, back—while Mama rests, feet heavy in his lap.

At the end of time there is no courtyard and no privy in the depths of the alley, hot and stinky, with the moist, broken door. No laundry to scrub and hang. Instead there is grass. I have seen grass; not felt it with bare feet, only gazed at the Central Forest as Mama moved us past—she said our kind could not get in, not unless we were working there—but I had glimpsed it, the trees, the green.

Inside the Central Forest, Yan says, creatures live in the ground, tiny things with lilting voices and stringy hair. The moon beams over the Forest and there are no gaslights. I want to go there, to live in the ground. At the end of time I imagine taking Yan's hand and entering the Forest, lounging with the grass between our bare feet and fingers. No need to wake up, no need to work.

Baba came from somewhere else. From the West, he said, on a long steam train full of men. Some kingdom—somewhere. Out west there were different trees and a roiling ocean, and the air smelled like cool salt, and the streets were muddy, not cobblestone, and there were no elevated trains.

At the end of time Baba comes back. Ng revives. The boy and girl twins turn brown and healthy and stop their cries. They open their eyes. Mama wakes up and Yan gets off her knees and we go to the Forest and press ourselves into the grass.

\*   \*   \*

Yan calls for me on Saturday morning. Sundays she goes to church, and nobody else in her family follows. Her parents clean buildings—on Sundays they work. I do not go to church; Mama does not believe. Mama said that Yan is sick in the head. Because she prays? Because she is a fool, Mama said. Yan can read words in the big book that she calls the Bible and I think that makes her smarter than me. There are different kinds of smart, Mama said. You are one and Yan is the other and you are the kind that counts.

Yan once tricked me into coming to the Rescue Society, said she knew there was a place to get food and coffee, that it was free for children. That there were good people who wanted to give free things to children like us just because they were nice. I knew better; I knew of tricks, but I was cold and the thought of coffee made me stupid. In the church basement we went to the tureen and gulped down the coffee, cup after cup, steaming hot and so sugary sweet I nearly gagged. Then we had to kneel and pray. My knees grew sore and I tasted the coffee for days, scraping the bits left behind on my tongue with my front teeth.

After the Rescue Society, Yan gave up on making me go to church. On Saturday evening we sit on the sidewalk with the younger girls, playing jacks. Mister Gumberd comes out of the apartment next door, dressed in his crisp collar and shiny shoes, mustache clipped and waxed. He whistles and pats his daughter Bessy, the one with the most jacks and the shiniest ball, on the head.

Bessy smiles and folds into herself, looking to the rest of us to make sure we are watching her. She waits to be watched.

My father, Bessy gums. Her eyes are blue and faded, her skin pink and flushed. How is your father? she asks.

Shut the fuck up, I say.

Shut the fud up, Bessy mimics. Have you seen your father lately?

I look at Bessy's pin curls and her tiny little teeth. She bounces her ball, a flip of the hand. I reach out and snatch it.

Hey! she shouts.

Yan looks at me and I can see her dry lips moving in prayer. I take Bessy's ball and hurl it into the street.

Bessy stands up. You go get my ball, she commands.

Get it yourself, I say.

Yan clutches my arm and I can hear her shallow breathing, know I will have to comfort her later, that she'll scold me in her thin voice for stealing. But I know how I am. I want to break people and spit in their faces and pull their hair. I want to lick their cheeks and bite their earlobes and feel their chins hard against my neck. When men pinch my bottom and poke me between the legs on crowded trolleys, I step on their toes; I dig my elbows into their guts. Picture their faces cracked open like split pumpkins on the trolley tracks.

I feel a weight on my shoulder, a warmth.

Girls, says Eletha.

One hand on Yan's shoulder, another on mine. On the corner, a horse and buggy is waiting.

Let's go, she says. We'll be late.

She ushers us into the buggy, settles in behind us.

Good day, the driver says.

We move away from 644th Street as Missus Gumberd comforts Bessy on the steps and they point at us, at me and Yan and zafty, beautiful Eletha, talking about our evil and our filth, how our kind should not grace even the rear buildings, or the rear yards within the rear yards. Wave goodbye, girls, Eletha says, gripping our shoulders so tightly her fingers dig into bone. And be sure to smile.

That is how we look as we leave: Eletha's thumbs jammed into my and Yan's bony shoulders, turning us to face the front of our building, all three of us waving with toothy smiles, mine and Yan's forced and tight, Eletha's also tight and false but practiced enough that it appears to strange eyes as something natural, soft. The driver hums and the horse raises its fine, sleek flanks and the buggy wheels begin to turn and we wave and smile and wave.

Yan is crying. She is an ugly crier, big gulps and whinnying squeaks, but Eletha doesn't soothe her or tell her to stop. Eletha sits tall as the horse and buggy shakes down the Boulevard. She is chewing gum that smells spicy. My mouth waters. I want to ask her for gum but I am afraid to speak, as if it will make her realize that we are here and should not be here, as if she will change her mind and take us home instead of wherever she is taking us. The Central Forest passes by on one side of the road, but we don't go in.

We turn onto a grand avenue full of large houses that I have never seen. Gaslights hum, and the street is empty and clean, cobblestones sparkling as if they've each been polished by hand. Maybe that is someone's job—like Yan's parents, who clean floors and walls and privies—a woman who squats in the street with a cloth and rubs the stones until they shine beneath the moon.

Have you been following me? Eletha asks. She wears a dark green hat with a brown feather tucked into its side, the feather as big as the hat itself.

Me and Yan flap our lips like dying fish.

Speak up, Eletha says. I can't hear you.

Me, I say. Me, not she.

Eletha looks at me at last. Her face is more beautiful up close, the square teeth, heavy eyelids, the nose long and strong with a bump on its tip. Her eyes are a gray color, and the green of the hat makes the insides glow.

Yes, she says, satisfied. I've seen you. She says my name.

Right, I say. And this is Yan.

So you are following me?

Not tonight. We were playing outside.

Playing my ass. I saw that Gumberd hussy about to beat you. She can eat shit.

I laugh. Yan turns away.

Eletha repeats, That Gumberd hussy and her worthless father would've had you thrown into the Tombs if I hadn't come along. Right?

Where are we going? I ask her.

The feather bobs. You'll see.

I look out the side of the buggy. The Tender Loin, Yan whispers, gripping the seat. I never told her what I saw when I followed Eletha last time, or that I had followed Eletha in the first place.

This isn't the Tenderloin, girls, Eletha says. She gestures out the window at the grand homes, their tall windows and heavy curtains. See, they have electric lights here.

Where is the jewel, I say.

What jewel? You got jewels?

You went inside a jewel.

Hush, Yan says.

I never went inside a jewel, Eletha says. I wish I lived in a diamond or a ruby. Imagine that? That your house was a big diamond. She draws this last word into three.

The buggy turns and I think about the places we could be going. To the docks, where Baba once warned me never to go. There were gangs there, oyster mongers who carried hatchets in the front of their pants. To the water.

Last summer, at the bathhouse on Rivington, Yan and I jumped into the water. It felt so cool, and as I went under I screamed with pleasure because my feet did not reach anything solid, only rippled beneath me. Baba had seen and had swum in the ocean out West, and at the bathhouse what I thought would be an endless bathtub was more like the world turned to liquid. I went under and the water filled my mouth. I bobbed up, spitting. I felt Yan's hands on my wrists, her legs wrapped around my waist. Slowly, we bobbed together. Yan's hair, wet and thick, dripped into my mouth, and for a moment it was only me and her, and I could hear nothing but her breathing, slow and warm, and my breathing, slowing to match hers, until a lady reached in and grabbed my hair and told us to get out. You cannot be here, she said. Go home, she said. Devils, she called us. Yan and I left, dripping and shivering. We ran to the El and stayed silent all the way uptown.

The buggy turns onto Fifth Avenue, moving through the crowds on a street of pushcarts and nickelodeons. It squeaks to halt in front of the building Eletha entered on the day I followed her on the El. The driver walks around to offer his hand to Eletha. Yan and I jump down ourselves.

I think of the sweet coffee. Are you taking us to pray? I ask, but Eletha laughs. Pray?

There's nothing wrong with praying, Yan says.

I hear before I see. The men, the wide black door, and the music, rolling, swaying, organs and violins and other instruments I do not know the names of. *Thump-thump-thump*, the music goes, *thump-thump-thump*. The men part and this time they do not stop me. With Eletha, Yan and I can go inside. Eletha swings as she walks, like her feet are thumping and the floor is rolling. I do the same; I must. So skinny I am but still I swing and sway to the music as it swells, as if I had big hips and big skirts, as if I were a big, fine lady with a horse and driver and a wad of gum that is spicy. I'm a girl, Yan yells over the music, we have to go home. No, I say. Yes, she says. No, I say. I aim for the lights and music like an arrow, Yan behind me. I hear the music. I see the lights.

Inside is a grand room, a hall with no windows, and the walls are covered with soft, pillowy fabric, purple and black and red and fuzzy all over, and the ceilings are tall and covered in lights—electric lights, steadily winking, and tiny flickering candles in brassy holders. Up in front is a band, men playing the piano, drums, horns, violins, and dressed in identical black suits. They play, stiffly hammering and blowing, and nobody watches them, because they are watching one another. The floor is shiny and smooth and the air smells like sweet smoke. There are mirrors hanging on the walls, and Yan gapes into one, studying her eyes and cheeks and hair, rubbing her face with her fists as if this will bring her into even clearer view, although this is the clearest view either of us has ever had of our own face, shinier and larger than in the cracked piece of glass Mama has nailed to the kitchen wall, or in the reflections in windows on sunny days. I do not want to look at my face, with its smudged chin and crooked hair, do not want to measure myself against the others.

The dancers dance one-two-three, one-two-three, one-two-three; they sweep and twirl around the room; couples and people alone, sliding and stepping, turning and twisting, thickening the air. I edge myself closer to the floor, leaving Yan with her mirror. Eletha dances with a woman with bright red hair and then switches to twirl with a bald man with chubby cheeks. She reaches out a hand. I take it. The chubby-cheeked man takes my other hand. And we are dancing, me between them, pulled on both sides, step-step-step, turn-turn-turn. Eletha throws me back and I fall into the lights and the whirling, and the man holds me and we sway together.

The song ends and Yan is there next to me, telling me with her eyes that she wants to leave. The chubby-cheeked man says, Welcome. To Eletha he says, Wherever did you find them.

Their families live in my neighborhood, Eletha says.

There are some like that, he says. Celestials living among the rest of us.

They can't go to school, Eletha says. They won't let them.

The bastards, the man says.

Hello, I say.

To Eletha, he says, She speaks!

The band begins again, and this time the beat is slower, steadier, a one-two, one-two, one-two, one-two kind of song, with sprinkling top notes, and the men and ladies begin to sway and sing, their voices raw and throaty. I do not know what I am supposed to do but I feel Eletha push me and say, Go dance, now. She pushes Yan by the shoulder blades. Go, dance.

Eletha and the chubby-cheeked man sway but do not move their feet. Yan and I dance. In the center of the singing men and ladies, we lift our knees and feet stiffly, elbows out, the look on Yan's face not one of joy but one of work, as if she is not enjoying this at all. We are the only ones dancing. Eletha watches us, the crowd cheering louder, and I am not enjoying this at all. Ho! Ho! shouts Eletha as she claps, the chubby-cheeked man's face redder, his belly a balloon.

Yan makes a run for the door but I grab her first. Her hands in my hands, her sweaty, knuckly smaller hands. The music is playing and we tumble onto the sidewalk, where I grip Yan harder and I am spinning her, and when I look at her I think she is scared and her mouth dangles open and I can't hear if she is laughing or crying or screaming, but when I look at her eyes I see that they are shining. We spin in circles until I am dizzy, flushing, and the streetlights are like lightning and I smile, laughing because I cannot do anything but laugh, as if laughing were as easy as breathing. I wonder if this is what Yan feels like when she is praying.

I last saw Baba in the morning. Hat on sideways, whiskers matted to his face. He was wearing saggy black pants and a saggy black jacket. I'm going to work, he said, and I watched him move across

644th Street with his black clothing, back rounding, face aimed at the ground. I felt needles in my throat. He stood, a small man, and turned to face me. See you soon, daughter, he said.

Then Yan and I are still and breathless. The El costs money and we have none. There is no horse and buggy waiting. I sink onto the sidewalk and Yan says, Come on, let's go.

How will we go, I ask. It's so far.

She says, We'll walk.

All the way to 644th Street?

We can stop when we want. We can rest if we need to.

I can't, I say. Let's go to the water. Let's go lie down in the Central Forest.

Yan pulls on me and says, Let's go home.

I get up. We hold hands, walking the first lonely block. I ask her to tell me a story about the things I've forgotten, ask if she remembers anything at all.

# FOUND PAPER, SOOT

*by* ANDREW MARTIN

I DROVE TO BOSTON on the Monday morning before the New Hampshire primary. The class I was teaching met from 4:30 to 6:50, and I had not anticipated how much the time of day would dictate the mood of the semester. The meetings started with nervous, unfocused energy that slowly splintered into malignant listlessness, my own manic volubility growing in direct proportion to my students' retreat. What a time to gather! I met with them in the bleak gap between coming home from work and preparing dinner: happy hour in a school full of burgeoning alcoholics. The gloom crept over all of us as the sun faded, and by the end of the class, it might as well have been the middle of the night, nothing awaiting us but the deep, cold northern darkness. I think the students respected my effort, even as they disregarded my broader purpose. I respected this disregard.

Six months after moving to New York from Boston, I'd found myself back there, teaching once a week for the spring semester, sleeping on friends' couches the night before or after class. I was working—improbably, or, perhaps more accurately, as fate demanded—at the university where my parents had met as under-graduates, and from which my brother had barely earned enough credits to graduate between semester-long blackouts. I'd been encouraged to apply directly to the chair of the department on the recommendation of a friend of mine who'd had to abruptly quit the week before the semester started, due to his own major alcoholic relapse. They'd needed someone fast; I was available, and my mediocre teaching résumé included no overt reports of grave misconduct. Even given these scrambled circumstances, when I got the job I'd worried that my father was somehow behind it, and despite his denials, I still couldn't quite shake the suspicion that this might have been the case. Perhaps it wasn't likely that main-taining a block of season tickets at the football stadium for two decades would carry much clout in the hiring of adjunct lecturers. But would it really *require* much clout to influence such a thing? There was nothing at this university more important than football, except for, nominally, Jesus.

I felt more hypocritical than I'd thought I would, teaching at a Catholic university. I knew it was mostly just for show, the priests in charge of things and the cross on the wall in the classroom, but still. I had gone out of my way to reject the arbitrarily cruel exer-cise of power that the Church represented, and it had come calling for me anyway. Maybe when you're raised Catholic, it always finds you. Whatever I was now, the Catholic stuff was a part of it, if not most of it. "Whatever I was now." Certainly not a model of service to the Lord. No traditional values, or at least none that I wasn't actively working to undermine, preoccupied as I was by sloth and gluttony and covetousness, et cetera. I had never worried seriously about hell—literal hell, I mean—outside of looking at Renaissance paintings and marveling at their inventiveness in conjuring demons and punishments. But I had spent most of my life feeling guilty for nothing. Or, guilty for things I'd done, some of which it seemed objectively correct to feel guilty about, others of which seemed wholly the product of a sin-centered upbringing. I'm not just talking about sex. But another thing about being raised Catholic is that one learns earlier than most that everything is, in fact, sex.

The class I was teaching was called Outsider Artists, though I had stretched the definition to include whatever I wanted to talk about. I wasn't a real art historian, but I'd written enough about art that my hiring was defensible, as long as it was only an "advanced writing elective" rather than, you know, an actual contribution to any known discipline. These were undergraduates from a random assortment of majors, fulfilling a writing requirement. It wasn't like they cared what I was trained in. Luckily, I was too arrogant to feel like a fraud.

My class that week was on the self-taught artist James Castle. A few months earlier, I'd seen his work for the first time, in a show at the Folk Art Museum, which, I hadn't quite realized, had been relegated to a glorified lobby in a building near Lincoln Center. The Castles were part of a grab-bag of an exhibition, one of those shows where the disparate interests of a particular collector are brought together because, well, the collector paid for it, I suppose.

Even among officially designated outsider art, Castle's work seemed to shy away from the crowd. It was eyeing the corners. Some of it was actually *in* the corner of the main gallery, and the rest looked like it wanted to be there. On rough paper, there were small, smudgy interior spaces and views of the world outside—a cast-iron stove in front of a vague approximation of wallpaper, the view from a barn of a farmhouse and silo. There was a rendering of a train, viewed frontally, giving it an ominous, anthropomorphic cast. There was a picture I loved of a group of totemic humanoids, lined up in a room like just-arrived aliens who have badly disguised themselves with ill-fitting human clothes.

All the pieces were titled *Untitled*, and all the dates were "n.d.," and the materials always included "found paper" and "soot." Castle had been deaf and mute, I read, and had lived his entire life with his family in rural Idaho. I felt myself immediately romanticizing him, his work and his story, even as I had barely the outline of it before me. The art was so dark and wise, so clearly tormented but lacking in self-pity. The pieces were stoic acknowledgments of the way things were, rigorous accountings of the immediate world. His pictures and people instantly meant something to me, I thought, because they lurked in their feelings in a way that I had been lurking in mine for some time. They expressed ambivalence in a more concrete way than an abstract painting could. They represented it, enacted the feeling of being caught between worlds, decisions, states of mind.

I tried to explain all this to my students, and they stared at me, politely enough, though without much sign of understanding or interest. Why had they signed up for this class? Maybe it sounded easy. Art history was, admittedly, easy. You looked at the pictures and you said what you thought you saw. That was what I had said in the first class, a little facetiously, obviously, and the students had seemed skeptical. They were right: when a person in a position of authority tells you something is easy, it is best to assume they are not telling the truth.

"I do get why these are cool," said Allison, a dark-haired young woman with big glasses. She was the kind of student that ill-prepared professors rely on, always finding something plausible to say no matter how doubtful the initial prompting. "But I guess I sometimes feel like technical limitations are also really, um, limiting. Like, how much of what we're noticing and finding interesting is just ineptitude that happens to be, um, aesthetically pleasing?"

"That, Allison," I said, "is the whole ballgame. It's kind of—"

"Alexandra," she said. "Sorry. Allie."

"Right, sorry," I said. I mixed up the names of all twelve women—only one male student had signed up for the class—constantly. "I was going to say that one way of looking at the whole development of artistic movements—*development* in quotes—is as a series of mistakes, of artists using their quirks and shortcomings to innovate and create something that has never been done before. I think this is what *The Anxiety of Influence* is about, probably. And sometimes that innovation, or whatever you want to call it, happens in the context of the broader conversation, and sometimes it happens in isolation. But then by disseminating these discoveries, we sort of *introduce* them into a narrative of progress."

*And thereby cheapen them*, Allie's eyes said.


I was supposed to have dinner with my friend Antonia after class at an old favorite bar on the Cambridge–Somerville border. She and I had spent many happy evenings there eating mediocre burgers and discussing Ellen Willis while watching regular-season Celtics games. The relative meaninglessness of the wins and losses was reassuring. As die-hard neurotics, we found it was easy in January and Februrary to talk ourselves out of too much excitement when the guys eked out a close one over a lesser opponent, or to find the silver lining in a blowout loss. (If they could play like that with Jaylen out, think how good they'd be when he was back!)

Antonia was waiting to hear about whether she'd gotten tenure at the prestigious university where she taught, the one right by Harvard Square. It seemed self-evident to me that she was a shoo-in. She was a brilliant writer, excellent at explaining things, and, conveniently, genuinely interested in postcolonial eco-literature. But what did I know. I'd gone to see her lecture once, to see if I could learn anything, and because I'd wanted to hear what she had to say about a popular recent novel in which the trees of the Brazilian rainforest gain sentience and fight back against their destruction and eventually lead a coup that, with the help of Indigenous tribes, overthrows the right-wing government. I knew she'd found the book facile and underwritten, and I was curious to see whether she would feign enthusiasm or excoriate it in front of the kids. What she did instead was far beyond my abilities as an educator. She walked the students through the novel step-by-step, pointing out the exciting things it did, why it was significant, what it echoed and possibly prefigured, while at the same explaining firmly why it was a disappointing and meretricious work of art. It was simultaneously generous and damning, all the more damning *for* being so generous. The kids seemed to actually be paying attention, too. Yes, many of them were on their computers, but their typing seemed coordinated with the rhythm of the information being disseminated, rather than totally random, like it was in my classes. Some of the students pushed back with their questions: Wasn't it possible that the book might be disrupting her Anglo-centric literary expectations with its use of dream logic and borrowings from ultraviolent contemporary cinematic conventions? Sure, Antonia responded, but what was it *doing* once it overturned those expectations? It was reinforcing aspects of the system that it was claiming to critique, no? The kids came back at her, and she opened up a new line of questioning: What *would* a novel that truly rejected these colonialist forms look like? Was such a thing possible?

No, the questions Antonia raised didn't blow my adult mind, but it occurred to me, possibly for the first time, that the point was not for her to entertain herself, or a visiting friend who was her age and of her level of sophistication, but to engage the youth and make them want to learn more. It was a delicate balance, one I had not found myself capable of maintaining. Despite my dabbling in higher education, the mysteries of academia only deepened with my further exposure to them. My pop-up, mostly improvised teaching gigs had very little in common with what Antonia did. But spending time with her at least made me feel more like the kind of person I imagined myself to be.

When my class ended, I walked in the bitter cold to my car on Commonwealth Avenue. I saw that while I'd been teaching, I'd gotten a text from Rebecca, my very recent ex-partner of many years.

"Hey, I'm really sorry to do this," her text read, "but I thought it should tell you as soon as I heard I got just got some really sad news. Sam Allard got hit by a car on her bike yesterday and I heard from Mike she died today. It's so fucking crazy and awful. I'm sorry. I hope teaching was OK. I'm so so sorry to do this."

I read it twice, hoping that somehow the typos and garbled syntax were concealing a less dire reality than the obvious one. They weren't. My instinct was to be angry with Rebecca. It was "just like Rebecca" to ruin a night I was looking forward to. Just like her to deliver terrible news that I did not want to have to grapple with or acknowledge. If not for her, Sam would still be alive—to me, at least—for a few more hours. *This* was exactly why we'd broken up.

Then, immediate remorse. Sam and I had been "see each other every week" friends for a couple of years in our twenties, in New York, but we'd remained "text when you see something funny that reminds you of the other person" close in all the years since, as we'd crisscrossed the country and ocean. We'd shared rental houses with friends, recommended each other for jobs, edited each other's work, both professionally and not. She was a wonderful friend and also a total flake, infamous among those who loved her for canceling a quiet hang in favor of a better party somewhere ("Wanna come? Can probably sneak you in somehow" was a classic non-invite). She demanded loyalty in feuds she instigated, once becoming furious with me for recommending a book in print by someone she was no longer speaking to for obscure reasons. She wrote mean reviews and profiles but was incredibly thin-skinned about any kind of criticism, professional or personal. She'd shown up in my hospital room in New York after I had my appendix out, taking a taxi directly there after flying in from Amsterdam. She hadn't come to the city just to see *me*, of course, but still. It was a great trick. She remembered birthdays, except when she didn't. She had a T-shirt that said RESPECT THE MEAT, the letters styled as flames, that she'd worn all the time. She really liked that second Lorde album with "Green Light" on it.

Sam. On her fucking bike. I'd told her to be careful, though I also obsessively warned everyone I knew never to ride a bike in any city, ever, which perhaps undercut my credibility on the subject. She'd been back in Brooklyn for the past year, but I'd only seen her twice since I'd moved back, and we hadn't had a chance to catch up properly. She was dating a guy for the first time in a while—she'd been seeing women for a few years, but after the last relationship ended badly, she'd told me she was "unwisely giving heterosexuality another chance." God, the loss. Another brilliant, secretly rich punk gone from the world.

"Oh no," I wrote back to Rebecca. "That's so awful. Thank you for telling me. I hope you're OK. Let's talk soon, yeah?"

It wasn't like anything I could say would be adequate, and I didn't want to talk on the phone. I didn't have room in my heart for Rebecca right now, didn't have the wherewithal to face her inevitable turn to my own heartlessness if we spoke. But still, it was a cold thing to do.

I texted Antonia to say I'd be a little late because I'd gotten some bad news. It was good to lay the groundwork; you shouldn't surprise people. I considered the possibility of not telling her what had happened. I didn't know if Antonia knew Sam, but she probably knew *of* her, and any chance for a night of light gossip and flirtation would go out the window if she knew I'd suffered a devastating personal loss. Was there any way to spin a lack of disclosure as shock and emotional self-protection rather than sociopathy? Probably for someone, but I think once the word *spin* has crossed your mind, the bet is off.

I followed the GPS on my phone through the back streets of Newton. I had lived in Boston for three years, but I still could not reliably find my way around anywhere, blindly relying on the computer to tell me how to get to places I'd been a hundred times. Which, whatever—why use any part of your brain for that, I guess. But I was in a self-castigating mood. I'd told a friend I'd drive with him to go knock on doors for Bernie in the morning. Now the idea of spending the day in the car with someone else, making small talk between running around in the cold on icy roads with no sidewalks, getting barked at by large dogs while people explained why they were voting for Tulsi fucking Gabbard, seemed even less appealing than it already had.

I found a parking spot only a couple of blocks away from the bar and walked quickly through the cold. Antonia was at a table in the front window, her head bent over a book, with a dark beer, barely sipped, on the table in front of her. I was even more glad to see her than I'd expected to be—grateful, even. I walked inside and she stood up to greet me, wrapping me in a tight hug. Her sweater was incredibly soft and she was wearing a pair of giant wire-framed glasses I'd never seen before. They made her face seem more delicate than usual, almost miniature.

"How are you?" she said. "What happened?"

"Oh," I said. "I... Rebecca texted and told me that a friend of ours died. It's just... I haven't even processed it yet. It's really terrible."

"Oh god, I'm so sorry," Antonia said. "Who... do you want to talk about who it was?"

"It's Sam, Samantha Allard? She's, you know, a writer and editor..."

"Oh fuck," Antonia said. "Fuck! Yeah, I know Sam. I *slept* with Sam. For a minute. Or. We were, you know, together. What *happened?*"

"She got hit by a car. On her bike. That's all I know."

"Jesus," she said. "We weren't, like, *close* lately, but we *were*. We spent just a *lot* of time together for a while."

I tried to imagine Sam and Antonia as a couple. Despite having, broadly speaking, the same vocation, they were fundamentally different in the way they approached the world, Antonia, methodical and intense, Sam, streaky and distracted and prone to sudden enthusiasms. I could only picture Antonia being exasperated with Sam, scolding her for not being more diligent about her career. Maybe that was part of it. But people were more complicated than that.

"She was kind of serially intimate," I said.

"Right," Antonia said. "I think I was the most important person in her life for, like, three months, and then just sort of *eh* after that. I don't *blame* her or anything. Obviously. I did miss her. This is awful. What do you want to *do?*"

"Well, drink," I said. "Eat? I need to eat at least. And, probably, cry. At some point."

Antonia checked her phone, frowning into the screen's white light.

"The texts are coming now," she said. "I'm really glad you told me first."

"I wish *no one* had told me first. Or at all."

"Right," Antonia said.

I got a beer and a "Crispy Southern Chicken Sandwich" that cost eighteen dollars. We fielded texts and updated each other on who was texting and tweeting and what they were saying. Mostly disbelief and sentimentality. The funny anecdotes and reposts of her pieces would come later. At least one person, someone neither of us knew, had already posted that Sam "would have wanted" people to vote for Bernie, which was, understandably, drawing pushback. If Sam were alive, she would have *voted* for Bernie, but I felt confident she wouldn't have guilted anyone about it, and even more confident that she was now well beyond caring who won a Democratic primary election.

Antonia and I ordered tequila and whiskey, respectively.

"I haven't been drinking like this," Antonia said. "It makes me sleep really badly. I wake up in the middle of the night with my heart pounding."

"Are you sure that's not happening anyway?" I said. "What with everything?"

"Yeah, to some extent. The booze definitely makes it worse, though. But. Desperate times."

"I just wanted to, like, talk about the Celtics," I said.

"Go ahead," Antonia said. "Looking solid but need better rim protection. Bench is inconsistent. Gordon Hayward is too white."

"It's true. It's all true."

"I feel so sad. I know plenty of people where it would be like, Okay, that makes sense. They lived hard. They had a, you know, a *doomed quality*. But Sam really didn't. I mean, she was kind of maddening, but she was mostly just, like, cute and funny and a good pal. This shit is just so deeply unfair."

I felt it too. Mortality had been creeping closer—a friend's brother from an overdose, a cerebral hemorrhage in a woman I'd gone to graduate school with. Even the death of Kobe Bryant, a player I'd never particularly liked, from a team I particularly disliked, had shaken me badly a couple of weeks before. It was the randomness of it all that made it vertiginous, the sense that one had been worrying about the wrong things. Somehow knowing that you would get it wrong didn't absolve you from worrying. It just made you feel worse for having wasted your time. Even though I hadn't seen her in months, I suddenly missed Sam's physical presence, the way she covered her mouth with her small, fidgety hands when she laughed, because of her crooked bottom teeth, the way she bobbed her head to some invisible beat when she was preparing to wholeheartedly disagree with you. Was there any footage of Sam to preserve these details? Maybe a glimpse of her in the background of a cat video? I didn't remember seeing any.

"Do you think it's especially...," I said. "Never mind, I shouldn't ask this."

"What?" Antonia sat up straighter, sensing a shift in tone. "You can ask anything. It's a wake."

"I was just thinking it might feel especially... something, when someone you had a relationship with dies. Had sex with, I guess. Like a particular kind of melancholy."

Antonia cocked her head slightly, like she was trying to decide whether she wanted to entertain this out loud.

"I don't know," she said. "I guess that makes it a little more sad, maybe. You always kind of think it might happen again. You might run into each other in a hotel lobby in a random city one day. I don't know why that's the fantasy. Something like that. You just lose, I guess, the future."

We drank quietly.

"You had a thing with her too," she said.

Somehow, despite the obvious sequential logic of the conclusion, it surprised me.

"Not really," I said.

Her eyes held mine.

"Well, it wasn't really anything," I said. "It was kind of secret. Because we were both with other people and it, ah, didn't ever become anything more significant. But, yeah. It was very, um, 'live while you're alive.' I think we both felt bad about it. And never really talked about it. And now I feel like an asshole."

Antonia took a sip of her drink and gave a quick, dismissive flick of the wrist.

"Oh, please, what, I'm going to judge you?" she said. "Whatever moral dimension there was is pretty, um, moot at this point. Was it fun?"

I thought about it. The tension had been fun, the vibrations in the air, the question of whether or not Something Was Going to Happen. Rebecca and I had been together at the time, but things were volatile between us. She was in San Diego for the bachelorette party of a friend she didn't particularly like—mostly, I thought egotistically, to avoid spending the weekend with me. Sam and I had been listening to records—*Tusk* and Tom Tom Club and *Lodger*—and getting quieter and heavier as the evening went on. I don't remember why she was in Boston in February. She had friends everywhere, nebulous "projects" that needed to be attended to. It was freezing out, and impossible to keep that apartment warm, because it was a converted attic and heating oil was insanely expensive. So we were layered and be-socked and still a little bit cold, but also glad to be inside, shielded against the elements with the dog, a unit united. Sam was going through a phase of digging up obscure movies from corners of the internet, and earlier in the night we'd watched a documentary filmed on the Wildwood boardwalk in the early '90s, featuring women of all ages speaking about their incredibly depressing expectations of love and pleasure. This had introduced a certain wayward romanticism to the evening, and also stirred intense teenage memories of my own time stalking the boardwalk in oversize T-shirts, excited by and fundamentally terrified of anyone remotely close to my own age, of any gender. Eventually, after much adolescent brushing up against each other, Sam made the first real move, as I am usually passive in such matters. Kissing her felt cathartic—finally, a conclusion to the narrative arc that had begun hours, if not years, earlier. It was an acknowledgment that the low-level flirtation I thought we'd been carrying on had not been entirely a projection. But that first kiss was the peak for me. I was a little bit too high and felt uncomfortable in my body, slow and awkward, and Sam seemed just the opposite, grabbing my hair, biting my lip, suddenly energized in a way she hadn't been before. She was all impetuous enthusiasm, and I felt outside of myself. We went to bed and had vigorous if unimaginative sex, then lay panting next to each other, neither of us having come. But once it was done—once we'd done all we could manage to do at the time, at least—I came back to myself, back to the moment, and felt all right. Sam was smiling unselfconsciously, hands behind her head in a cocky *just got laid* posture. "These kids!" she exclaimed. Meaning us, I guess. I didn't sleep at all, listening to every creak in the house, hearing the radio of every car that stopped at the red light on our corner. In the morning we both were awake early and had coffee and I walked her to the train station with the dog. I felt like I was using the dog as cover, as if it would be suspicious to accompany my friend to the train station without a chaperone. We talked, for at least the third time in twenty-four hours, about a couple we knew who were abruptly (to us) breaking up after ten years together, and how terrible it was going to be for everyone to figure out which one of them to invite to things now. She paused at one point in the conversation and said, "We're good, right?" I said, "Yeah, of course." And she said, "Cool." When I got home, I realized she'd gotten some blood on the sheets and I panicked—the telltale heart. No sin goes unpunished. Catholicism's revenge. Et cetera. I did the laundry and the sheets came out looking like all the other old fucked-up sheets we had. Rebecca had no questions. It made no difference.

"It was fun," I said. "It wasn't a very nice thing to do, though."

Antonia shrugged.

"You shouldn't worry about it," she said. "At this point."

She put her hand on mine and rubbed her thumb a couple of times over my knuckles, a touching combination of comforting and impersonal. I felt a new connection between us, different from what we'd had before, rooted in this particular strain of grief. We paid the bill and walked out into the cold. It was worse than it had been, or felt that way, at least, after being in the warm pub for so long.

"We didn't even talk about your tenure stuff," I said.

"Thank god," she said. "This whole thing... It's stupid to complain about it, but it's actually insane. My case is 'looking good,' supposedly, but I don't want to jinx it."

"You'll get it," I said. "I promise."

She raised her eyebrows, and it felt like the right thing to step forward and kiss her. My lips briefly made contact with hers, just long enough to taste a trace of tequila. She stepped backward and said, "Oh no!" in a voice that was trying to attain jocularity, maybe, but couldn't mask her panic.

"Ah," I said. "I think I got a little carried away."

"It's okay!" she said, more brightly than was called for. "It was just surprising. Not the, uh, not the vibe tonight. Don't worry about it!"

"I'm really sorry," I said. "I thought... I just thought something else."

"It's okay!" she said. "I'll see you soon."

She hugged herself and smiled faintly.

"Maybe if there's a thing for Sam," I said.

She looked at me as though she had no idea what I was talking about. I gave her a minute to walk away—my car was in the same direction she'd gone. I suddenly felt the accumulated alcohol in me and wished I could have the last few hours back. The last few years too. Everything I did took me back to the same place—Boston, right, yes. But also to *this*. Loneliness and trespass, one always leading to the other. I wanted to call Sam now, even though I hadn't called her in years. She would have given me shit for being self-dramatizing. If she could have. The people I could actually call now would almost certainly be less forgiving.

I found my car, steered it to Memorial Drive and out to I-90. I would skip the canvassing in the morning, tell them I'd decided to head home after all, that I was worn-out and needed to regroup. At this time of night, it would be less than four hours to my apartment in Brooklyn. I would make phone calls to New Hampshire, doing exactly as little good calling unanswered phones as I would have knocking on the doors of empty houses.

I thought about the Castle pictures I'd shown to my class, all those silent, ominous rooms and landscapes, the huddled gatherings of crude figures. It didn't seem like the kids had understood them, really. Maybe I hadn't explained the whole thing well enough—the inventiveness with limited materials, the persistence, the miracle of the work surviving at all. I hadn't given them enough context, or found a way to help them see the art for themselves. It was more about the feeling they evoked, I thought, than about the particulars. The melancholy of rendering things again and again to fix them in one's mind. Maybe they were still too young to feel the pathos of that. Or maybe, as Allison had suggested, the work itself wasn't as interesting as I thought it was. Alexandra, rather. Allie.

I reminded myself that they didn't have to feel what I felt— that wasn't the point. The point, supposedly, was that they learn something.

# TETHER

*by* CATHERINE LACEY

SHE OFTEN FOUND HERSELF walking a few paces behind him.

Though they would set out from their home together with the stated intention of walking in tandem in order to visit a certain café or dually attend to the grocery shopping or some other errand, and though their steps kept pace with one another for the first several minutes of this journey, as they discussed their days and ideas and impending social commitments, eventually a congenial silence would fall between them—the sort of congenial silence well known to pairs who've spent many years together—and it was during this silence, she had noticed, that his gait would slightly widen and quicken, and this new, impatient gait would soon carry him a full step ahead of her, then two steps, then several. Here the gap between them would hold steady, and for a long time they would travel along their shared path at the exact same speed. It was almost as if there were some invisible tether between the two that prevented him from going any farther ahead than those few steps. It was there that he would remain—several steps ahead of her—for the rest of their walk, if, that is, it could still be described as a walk they were taking together.

Are there any criteria, she thought while looking at the back of his handsome skull, that a walk must meet in order to be considered a walk taken together? Could two strangers who happened to be walking on the same path and at the same speed be said to be walking with each other even if there were many yards between them? Or did a pair need to be within grasping reach of each other in order to be sharing a walk? Did that pair need to be on speaking terms? Did they even need to know each other?

On they went like this—he ahead of her and she behind him— and she would eventually wonder what the two of them looked like to others on the street. Did they appear to be walking together? Did she seem to be following him? Did he seem to be fleeing her? Or did other pairs have this problem too? Was remaining just out of reach an integral agreement of marriage? Is there some important instinct that tells us to stretch that tether taut?

# HOW TO
# BECOME A STAR

*by* SANTIAGO RONCAGLIOLO

*translated by Joel Streicker*

"DON'T USE MY NAME. Or my family's. It could hurt my son. He doesn't want to remember any of this. I don't either, I guess."

The expression of the woman sitting in front of me oscillates between a polite smile and extreme anguish. We've met up at one of the best Japanese restaurants in Madrid, next to the Congress, but she doesn't want to eat. She says she only wants to talk. She's come to tell me a story. And it's a long one.

"In fact, don't publish what I'm about to tell you in my country," she continues. "Don't even say where everything happened. Let's say in some small country in South America. Ecuador. Or Paraguay."

It's not the first time I've had an encounter like this. Between 2007 and 2012, I published a trilogy of true stories, all of them written on a work-for-hire basis. Those three books turned into an unending source of problems: death threats, criticism, endless meetings with lawyers, campaigns against me in the press in various countries... and me, alone in my defense.

I believed that a newspaper story should defy silence: it should say things that others don't dare to say. I still believe this. Only now I include myself among the "others."

Despite my desertion—or my rehabilitation, depending on your perspective—I'm still known as a hit man of narrative: a writer who accepts stories as work-for-hire and is willing to get into trouble.

Every once in a while, some individual comes out of nowhere and contacts me to tell a far-fetched tale, in the hope that I'll write it up. I've been offered the story of an old millionaire who got into a fight with his children because he married his nurse; the memoirs of a Peruvian guerrilla who was in prison for a quarter century; and the biography of an obscure resident of Madrid who thought—a bit pathologically—that the entire history of Spanish democracy revolved around him.

I take those meetings, listen to those stories, and keep them for my private collection. Some of them aren't even stories. Their owners think themselves more interesting than they are. Even so, they just want to tell me their adventure. And I like to listen.

The woman today is named Ana. Or that's what I'll call her in this text. She's been seeking me out for more than a year—not because I've played hard to get, but because we live on different continents. During this time, numerous common acquaintances have insisted I listen to her story. And on this day at the end of fall, at lunchtime, we're finally in Madrid at the same time.

We've agreed on this restaurant because it's across the street from her hotel, the Westin Palace, which is one of the city's most expensive. Asking around, I've found out that she herself is the owner of a hotel chain in South America. At any rate, I order the cheapest thing on the menu. I still don't know who's going to pay the check.

"My therapist recommended I tell my story," she explains. "I'm not sure what for. I don't want a news story coming out. I'm terrified that everyone's going to know what happened. I've been thinking that maybe you could write a novel, with fictitious characters and false names."

If this person believes she's deciding what novels I write, I'm afraid we're both wasting our time. A novel is precisely the space where I write what I want, without bosses or pressures. It's my zone of freedom. But we're both here, and there's no need to get too theoretical. I order a glass of wine and settle in as if I were about to watch a movie. I say, "To find out, first I have to hear that story."

## MARTÍN

"My son, Martín, wanted to be a singer. He's my only child and that was the only thing he wanted. So I helped him. It's what a mother should do. I paid for his studies in our country and abroad, although he didn't finish them. Six years ago, when he was twenty-three, Martín started a heavy metal band called Estruendo. Music is a complicated business. And I asked myself: When should a person get his inheritance? When he's old and washed-up, and his parents are dead? I answered myself: No, it's better to give him his inheritance to finance his dream while he's still young. It's better to invest in his career and his happiness. It makes sense, right?"

Ana has ordered teriyaki chicken just to have something on the table, but she barely touches it. In fact, she doesn't like Japanese food, can't stand the idea of eating with chopsticks. While I devour a salad, her fork fossilizes on her plate, buried in a sauce that only gets thicker. She continues.

"I became an investor in Estruendo. I underwrote their first album and their first video. We wanted to do everything totally professionally."

While we talk, I search YouTube for the band's first video. The song is called "Fuera de sí." The video's director is local but pretty famous, pretentious, even. He won some MTV awards at the beginning of the 2000s. Then he announced on social media that he was leaving the country because he couldn't stand its media's "audiovisual garbage" any longer. He considered himself a citizen of the world, with a "universal consciousness," and couldn't continue living in a place where the public prefers what's "vulgar and cheap." Nonetheless, he still works with pop and rock bands from there.

The video is technically impeccable, well lit, and attractive, despite the wardrobe—Grand Prix motorcycle racing suits—which is a bit sporty for a metal band. The location is industrial: a brick factory, or something like that, appropriate for the song's paranoid-hyperactive atmosphere. In six years, it's received 146,463 views. It has 228 comments, most of them highly favorable, although there's a joke about the band's "Power Rangers" look, and a pair of scornful comparisons to kiddie rock.

Oh, and a troll who points out that, with the money the singer has, anyone could afford to make a video like that.

In addition, Estruendo has an official YouTube channel with 2,795 subscribers.

Ana continues:

"Of course, we hired a manager, except the manager was too… old-school. He waited around for people to call him to invite the group to give concerts, or get one of their songs on the radio. And things didn't work like that anymore. It was 2011. The world was starting to change."

Ana pauses dramatically while playing with the chicken that she has no intention of eating. I know an important fact is coming:

"Then Paula Pinter appeared: Paupi."

As if to emphasize Paupi's sudden appearance, the waiter brings me my makis. I can eat in peace. Ana prepares a long salvo of facts.

## PAUPI

"Paupi got in touch with us by email from AOL, a digital subsidiary of Time Warner in New York. AOL's entertainment division had launched TMZ a few years before, one of the leaders in information about celebrities, and they were looking for new stars to amplify their influence in the Spanish-speaking world. They'd seen Estruendo's video and found it promising. Actually, in Latin America, the only countries with decent show business industries are Mexico and Argentina, maybe Colombia a little. Aside from those places, AOL had a hard time finding talented and professional artists. That's why they saw a lot of potential in Estruendo."

As she proceeds to talk about this Paupi, it gets difficult for Ana to speak. I notice that she measures her words, and at times her eyes tear up. To get her to relax, I order a bottle of wine. Ana is grateful, and, cheered by the rioja white, she starts to talk about the changes the AOL executive introduced to the band.

According to her story, Paupi began asking about Estruendo's website, its Facebook profile, and its social media in general. Ana explained that they didn't have any of that, and Paupi was outraged.

"'Nowadays no one gets anywhere without social media!'" Ana imitates her. "'No one waits around for someone to call them anymore. Marketing is viral now. Bands communicate directly with their followers. They create followers through their computers. That's where the future is.'"

Time has shown that Paupi was absolutely right. And of course she knew what she was talking about: AOL had been in the digital business since its beginnings. But, apart from that, she firmly believed in Estruendo. She offered to personally, and for no charge, monitor the work of the boys' social media. And, in a quite natural way, while she was carrying out all this work, she became Ana's friend.

"Paupi was a very brave woman. She left Venezuela during the

Chávez years because there was no future for her there. And she started from zero in California, where she quickly became a social media guru. Now, despite her international success, she followed events in Venezuela, took part in social media campaigns against the regime, and waited for the moment to return to her country to help it move forward."

Following her advice, Martín opened a Facebook page to promote the group and made some efforts on social media. Unfortunately, Paupi rejected everything he proposed. Martín wasn't a professional. He was a musician. His management of social media projected an amateur image of the group, as if it were a band made up of neighborhood friends. And he didn't know how to produce something viral. If Estruendo wanted to attract attention beyond its national borders, it had to overcome very professional competition that had years or even decades of experience in the industry. In short, they'd need a real digital strategist.

"Once again, she was right... But who was going to do that? That job didn't even exist. Our country was just starting out. No one had done viral marketing for a rock group before. No one had even thought of doing it."

Luckily, Paupi had contacts all over. She located a man who did social media for the successful Mexican pop group Reik. It seemed like the guy did very good work. And the most important thing was that he lived in the same country as Ana.

And that's how Hugo Cuesta came into the picture.


### HUGO

"Paula Pinter recommended me? What an honor!"

Hugo Cuesta considered Paupi one of the greatest digital communications leaders. He had no idea that she knew his work, and he felt very proud when he found out.

In his introductory interview with Ana and Martín, he showed them all the work he'd done for Reik: social media, YouTube, website. He explained his secrets to them, which, back then, were still fairly unknown: hashtags, followers, likes. He was willing to do the same for Estruendo, although he made it clear that, at least at the beginning, the Mexicans were his priority, and he'd have to travel a couple of times a month to take care of them. Nobody saw anything wrong with that. On the contrary, that meant having a foot, or at least a toe, in the door of the all-powerful Mexican music industry.

"The difference with Hugo was apparent from the start," Ana recalls. "He had a really strong impact on their image. The group's followers multiplied. The next step was to gain fans by performing live at the few festivals our country had. And, of course, to start to think about their next work."

They recorded the second album in Buenos Aires. For the video, they hired the same director as they had for "Fuera de sí." But the style was harder and more sophisticated. The new single, "Círculo del infierno," sounds like nu metal. Their wardrobe is glossy black, with a mask for the guitarist along the lines of Slipknot or Buckethead. And the claustrophobic aesthetic is reminiscent of Tool's videos, with disgusting worms crawling on the ground, and a naked, dirty, frightened vampire.

Without a doubt, the viral strategy worked. On YouTube, many of the 312 comments state that they'd come to view the video because of publicity from the platform. And in three years, the views had risen to almost two million. Three times as many as "Fuera de sí" had, and in half the time. But it wasn't all good news.

"At that point, Paupi had to disconnect a little from the band. We stayed in friendly contact, but she was changing jobs. Google had hired her for its London office, so she no longer had a direct relationship with Latin American artists. And, as if that weren't enough, she spent long stretches in Venezuela collaborating on the communications strategy of the resistance, which was starting its battle against Nicolás Maduro. At any rate, she supported us however she could: she asked her show business friends to advise us pro bono, just because of their personal relationship with her. The most entertaining one was Etienne Daguereau, a French stylist who would write to me in terrible English because he was studying the language and wanted to practice. He had very good taste. And he was charming."

While he traveled between Paris and Miami to dress stars on both sides of the Atlantic, Daguereau formulated for Estruendo a whole stylistic portfolio that included not only their wardrobe but facial creams and hair products. As he explained, a band's videos should be designed to be projected on giant screens, where any skin imperfection will appear magnified.

Some of the clothing Daguereau recommended could be gotten on the cheap in the informal markets in his country, a mix of counterfeit brands and decent-quality imitations. But the cosmetics could be bought only in their original version, and they were pretty expensive.

"I tried to ask for help from the parents of the other musicians, but there was no way. The only one who could finance those things was me. At least a lot of the domestic flights could be bought with credit card points. That was a small savings."

At this point in the story, I can't help asking:

"Three years. Two albums. Two movie-quality videos. Styling. Tours. How much had you spent by that point?"

Lunch is over. In theory, we share a tea mousse, but Ana barely touches it.

"I'd prefer to keep that information to myself," she says.

*   *   *

## DORIS

Although Paupi had changed companies, AOL maintained its objective of expanding its markets in Latin America. The new regional director's name was Doris Barnechea, and her family was from Cuba. And although her manner was colder and more impersonal than that of her predecessor, she always kept in touch with Ana.

Ana, for her part, was enthusiastic. Now that Estruendo had a second professional-quality album, it was time to begin planning the international rollout.

"Doris didn't waste time telling me about her life," recalls Ana, who, in the end, pays the check. "She only thought about work. She constantly asked us for market reports, publicity materials, target demographics, statistics, numbers, data... The problem was that she didn't have time to explain exactly what form she wanted the information in or how we should organize it. She was used to working with people who already knew everything. So I drafted and sent her documents nonstop, which she invariably returned saying, 'This isn't what I asked for'; 'Where are the breakdowns of the target audience by age?'; 'I need an overall profile, not a media plan.' It was frustrating."

Music groups, writers, and artists are—for their recording companies, publishing houses, or galleries—commercial products. And like any product—hot dogs, aspirin, aerosol deodorant—a lot of information must be coordinated before they can go on the market. Only, once again, their country had no experience with this kind of merchandise. Neither Ana nor anyone in the group knew of anyone who could take charge of all these reports and materials.

Fortunately, Estruendo was beginning to extend its tentacles beyond the domestic market. Even so, Hugo Cuesta, the digital strategist, continued working with Reik. In fact, he was working more and more with them, as the launch of their new album, *Des/Amor*, approached. Reik had been successful for ten years, and they had a whole team of specialists in marketing and analysis. Hugo offered to ask this team to help prepare the information Doris asked for. And they agreed.

The Mexican advisers—Juancho and Sole—turned out to be as nice as Paupi. They were a couple in the process of getting divorced, and Ana wound up listening to all their complaints and mediating between them. But, unlike Paupi's friends, these new partners wouldn't work for free.

Nonetheless, they didn't try to bleed the group dry. Their fees were pretty reasonable for the amount of time they worked. Besides, because Hugo traveled constantly to Mexico City, he could take the payments in cash, avoiding bank commissions and double taxation. After taxes were eliminated, the fees came out to what a friend would charge.

"At first, I'd thought about setting up Estruendo as a company. But we only had expenses, no income. Incorporating, keeping books, paying a financial manager would've only led to more expenses."

With or without a formal company, Juancho and Sole seemed very professional. As soon as they came on—with their perfect graphics, their precise information, and their weird words in English—Doris accepted all the documents without complaint, and she passed them along to her bosses with high praise for the efficiency of Estruendo's management.

Then things started rolling with AOL. The executives showed interest. Their teenage daughters, according to Doris, were crazy about the two videos. The band was jumping at warp speed through all the hoops for its international launch.

And finally, after years of effort, the email arrived that we'd been waiting for: with great fanfare, Doris announced that the company's scouts would go see Estruendo live, in the flesh, without any more intermediaries.

### THE CONCERT

"It couldn't be just any gig in a bar. Doris was clear on that point. The scouts had to see Estruendo on a big stage, with the best sound, seducing a massive audience. The group had to kill."

Now Ana and I are walking along the Paseo de Recoletos, at the edge of the Prado Museum and the Royal Botanic Gardens, toward the Atocha station. Everything around us is European and ancient, so Ana's story seems to have occurred on a very distant planet, at some point in the future.

"In my country, the rock industry doesn't exist. No one pays bands to play at festivals, for example. On the contrary, the band winds up paying for the techs, all the expenses. I moved heaven and earth to get the group into the top festival in the capital. It seemed impossible, but I managed to do it. They would play with the country's premier bands, although they'd open the show. It would be best for the scouts to arrive on time. I would've sent them a taxi, a limousine; I would've put them up or invited them out to eat. But Doris explained that scouts don't work like that. They are like food critics: they work incognito."

Estruendo prepared thoroughly for that date. New clothes, polished instruments, improved songs. The band's sound was tight as clockwork. Optimism reigned supreme.

Maybe too much optimism. Because it's never possible to control everything. There's always some detail missed, some part of the ship's rigging that gets tangled.

"The day of the concert, when the boys got onstage, the feedback didn't work. The musicians couldn't hear themselves! They thought the techs would fix the problem, and they forged ahead. The sound was a nightmare. They lost the beat. They were out of tune. After a few songs, the sound guy announced that they'd have to reboot the mixing console. Then Martín, who is terribly shy and hates speaking in public, had to fill fifteen minutes with a disjointed discourse in front of all those people. Horrible. Finally they fixed the sound. They played again. Now they were perfect. The second half of the concert was spectacular. But, of course, no one hires you for half a concert."

Predictably, the scouts didn't come up to talk with them after the set. In the wake of this failure, the band's depression lasted for weeks. The group had bet its future on a single card, and it had turned out to be a joker. The project was on the ropes. The musicians asked themselves if it was worth it to continue. As if that weren't enough, Martín had a new girlfriend, who was pressuring him to go solo. She believed that Estruendo was a drag on his talent. Ana didn't like the new girlfriend at all. But she wasn't sure what to do next.

"Then the story took a new turn. A completely unexpected one. When we were thinking we'd burned all our bridges, Doris Barnechea got in touch again."

Ana doesn't recall each conversation; she relives it. She narrates the facts with the passion of a schoolgirl talking with her first boyfriend. When she speaks, it's clear that Estruendo wasn't just her son's dream. It was hers.

"Doris said she was sorry it had taken her so long. On the other hand, it was logical: they'd just held the Grammys, which, evidently, always involves a lot of promotional and distribution work. Now things were calmer, and she finally had time to relay the scouts' verdict. It turned out they understood about the technical problems. None of that bothered them, because if AOL was going to promote an artist, it would guarantee optimal sound and lighting conditions. The problem, actually, was something else. Something deeper."

Now we are passing by the used-book sellers along El Retiro Park. The sun is falling on the bookstalls and the pedestrian walkway. It's one of those days when it seems nothing bad can happen.

"The AOL people expressed doubts about Martín's voice. Not because he sang badly. It was a question of the texture of his voice.

For heavy metal, you need a more guttural timbre. He didn't have it. It lacked power, and at the same time it was too sweet and too high. According to the experts, Martín's voice could be successful... But he'd have to devote himself to Latin pop."

### "PIENSO EN TI"

Estruendo's last video is a planetary leap more than a change of style. No more distorted guitars. It's a very romantic ballad called "Pienso en ti." No more masks or paranoid sets. Just a simple and ordinary story about an office romance, with its obligatory sex scene. No more futuristic wardrobes. Martín wears a casual shirt and rides a bike. No more lyrics about vampires and insects. The chorus says, "I don't want you to leave, and with you, your scent from my sheets."

"Groups evolve. Right?" Ana says in defense of the changes. "This could also be a creative shift for Estruendo."

Now we're sitting in El Retiro Park, drinking coffee and Coca-Cola in front of the monument to the fallen angel. A serpent wraps itself around the angel's legs while monstrous gargoyles spit water into the fountain. The statue is an omen. Or a warning. About what happens when you aspire to be more than what you are.

Initially, the "Pienso en ti" video didn't do badly: 549,876 views in the first year. Although something strange happened afterward. Or, rather, something was interrupted. According to YouTube, there existed another video from that album, "Miénteme," that had been withdrawn from the platform. And "Pienso en ti" itself has only twenty-nine comments. Some are from old metal fans disappointed by the band's shift. The last comment cruelly returns to the theme that the singer's family has a lot of money, and that's why no one says how bad the video is. At that moment, at any rate, the music wasn't the only important thing. Stranger things were happening.

On the outside, in the corporate universe, everything was in motion. Now Ana was in the process of sending gifts to influencers, big music stars, so they'd vote for Estruendo at the next Latin Grammys and would recommend that their colleagues vote for Estruendo, too. Of course, those people don't accept cheap gifts. Attracting their attention required offering gifts that stood out: a handbag with artisanal silverwork for Shakira. Baccarat crystal glasses for Maná. A Rolex for Carlos Vives. Hugo sent the gifts along with a CD of the band through his contacts in Mexico and Miami. Often, he bought them himself, and Ana reimbursed him.

But while the promotional machine seduced the stars, the band began to show unexpected weaknesses. The most serious: Martín didn't want to sing. He was suffering from depression. Before traveling to a concert, in the middle of the airport the leader of Estruendo announced that he wouldn't get on the plane. He said he was experiencing an attack of stage fright. This happened a few times.

Martín wasn't focusing at rehearsals, either. He'd show up late. Or he wouldn't show up at all. Or he'd show up drunk after partying with his girlfriend in the middle of the afternoon. He'd always worked with a lot of discipline, but suddenly he was losing his desire and his faith in the band.

In her role as manager, Ana began to get angry with him and demand more commitment. But her managerial role got mixed up with her role as his mother. Martín was now too old to let his mother police his partying. But, nonetheless, he lived at home. Their fights multiplied. Maybe the time had come to change the project. The band's dissolution and Martín's moving out were beginning to seem possible.

And then, when everything looked like it was the predictable end of a cycle, the devil came on the scene. Nothing less.

## THE PURSUIT

"One day, Hugo Cuesta brought me a horrible piece of news: my son's girlfriend was planning to kidnap him. And he showed me the proof."

By this point, everyone on the Estruendo team knew that Hugo Cuesta was a hacker. Not only did they know it: it was part of his work. Hugo went into the Facebook and Instagram accounts of the group members for quality control, to make sure no one posted inappropriate comments or images. He even slipped into their WhatsApp. And that's where he saw a conversation between Martín's girlfriend and another man, someone nobody in the band knew.

The dialogue, which Ana printed out and brought me, leaves no doubt about their intentions:

HER: Saturday I take Martín to the party and get him drunk.
HIM: That's it. And when you leave, I'm on him.
HER: You're not going to hurt him. Huh?
HIM: I only want the 🔫 The thing is to convince the family to give it
    up quick and without calling a 👮♂
HER: I'll handle that. I love you.
HIM: ♂ 🖤
HER: But also 🔫

From here, the story took on a totally new tenor. If the change in the band's style was outrageous, what happened next made that look like a trifle.

"I found a really strange drawing under my bed. A kind of star with symbols added on it. I looked on the internet and found out it was a satanic design. And the worst part is that more began to appear, in the garden, in the kitchen, all over the house. Whoever left them there either had access to our life or they pulled off some kind of powerful magic."

Ana is Catholic. Hugo himself had accompanied her to Mass once. She had a certain inclination to accept that in life there are malignant forces at work. Martín didn't. He didn't believe anything Ana told him. Everything sounded to him like superstitions and hoaxes. But then he started getting photos on his phone of their own house that could only have been taken from a drone. Someone was watching him. Satanic or not, his pursuers weren't amateurs.

"I got Hugo to investigate our communications, with no limits. He was the only one who could help us. And he came to the conclusion that a sect was planning to kill Martín and me. The girlfriend was only part of a wider plan of destruction."

The plan, according to Hugo, was to get rid of them imminently. Terrorized, Ana and her son fled to the jungle on the first flight they could catch. From there they maintained contact with Hugo, who had detected their pursuers via GPS.

"It was horrible, like a science fiction thriller. We stayed at a hotel, and we got word that the killers were coming after us. Hugo even showed me their movements on a geo-location map. We snuck away and returned to the capital incognito. I asked a friend to put us up at her house so no one would know where we were. I told her I couldn't explain why. Just that we needed a hideout. She took us in. I spent a couple of days in her guest room, with the phone off, taking sleeping pills. Later, when she noted that I was calmer, she asked me: 'Ana, what's going on? Trust me. Tell me.'"

Despite suffering intense paranoia at this point, Ana confided in her friend and explained everything in great detail, just like she would explain it to me a year later. She had to explain who was pursuing her and how she knew it. That led her to talk about Hugo and, therefore, about Paupi, who had recommended him in the first place. And, in the end, she narrated the whole adventure of Estruendo and its characters.

We've walked over to an open-air café in the Retiro, near the rose garden. Ana has ordered another Coca-Cola. Her face has been tensing up, not from fear or fury, but from stupefaction. She continues:

"The husband of this friend is a lawyer. She wrote down all the information I gave her about the payments, the emails, the dates, and she took all that data to her husband's office. There, they investigated everyone, while I rested in their house. I still didn't dare turn on the phone, but the human contact made me feel better. Three days later, the husband said he had something to tell me. He asked me to sit. He offered me tea. What he said to me next was the last thing I was expecting to hear, and it turned my life upside down: 'We've looked for all the people that you've communicated with. And they don't exist. The emails they send you don't come from real addresses at AOL or Google. The executive positions they claim to have were never created. There's no stylist that goes by Etienne Daguereau. In fact, even the name Hugo Cuesta is invented.'"


### THE AWAKENING

"For five years, I lived inside a novel. I communicated with fictional characters. But they were so real… Paupi and her anti-Chavista activism. Etienne and his English classes. The Mexicans and their divorce. I'm incapable now of explaining how I believed everything. I don't understand how they brainwashed me. The fact is that I became these people's friend. I shared everything with them."

Among all those friends, the only flesh-and-blood human was Hugo Cuesta. A few days after the discovery, he appeared at Ana's house, supposedly out of concern for her. Ana would've liked to slap him, but she didn't even know what she could concretely accuse him of. And she feared what he might be able to do with whatever she told him.

"I said I felt bad, that I couldn't talk to him now. I'm certain he sensed that something was up with me. He told me: 'You seem cold. What's wrong? Don't you want us to work together anymore? And what's going to happen to Estruendo? It's your dream.' I told him I'd call him. That same day, I suppose, he erased all the databases, emails, communications. Paupi, Doris, Juancho, Sole, and ten more characters disappeared forever."

Ana sent detectives to investigate that damn Hugo Cuesta. It turned out he was a computer tech, the graduate of a cheap academy, like millions of her countrymen. He lived in a working-class neighborhood. He'd never traveled to Mexico. Not even his name was real.

She wanted to destroy him in court, but her lawyers explained that there was nothing to sue him for, because he hadn't taken anything from her. She had paid his salary, of course, but in exchange for work managing social media, which had been carried out properly. The same with the man at the recording studio, the video director, the sound engineers. Ana could file a claim about the money sent to the Mexicans or the gifts to the big stars, but all of that had been done under the table to avoid taxes and commissions. They turned out to be impossible to verify.

What Cuesta stole wasn't money. He stole the universe of glamour that he himself had created for her. Or maybe not. Maybe his true work, the service he sold, was inventing that universe.

The scam's accomplices didn't exist even virtually. The only evidence that remains of them are those sheets of paper with their data and a few printed text exchanges, which Ana won't allow me to take home. When it comes down to it, aside from the videos on YouTube, I myself have no evidence that her story is true.

"I'm still trying to understand why Hugo did all that," she concludes. "Just to keep a job? I don't think so. I suppose it was for my son. I think he liked Martín. And they became very good friends...

or that's what Martín believed. He's the one who was harmed the most. He says they've ruined his life. That they made him believe he had talent, when, really, he's a nobody. Don't call him to ask about all this. He doesn't like to remember it."

It's night when I say goodbye to Ana. I promise her I'll write the story, in spite of all the limitations involved. I'll publish it in a country far from her own. If possible, in another language. When I leave her in the café, we're both in a reflective, almost melancholic mood.

Heading out from the Retiro, on my way to the Atocha station, I pass by the monument to the fallen angel again. The streetlamps are now lit, and under their ghostly light, the gargoyles appear to see me off with a mocking smile.

# LONG
# BLACK SOCKS

*by* STEPHANIE ULLMANN

THEO IS LOOKING FOR a pair of long black socks. Apparently, it isn't easy to find long black socks in Beijing in 1989. Theo's father wanted to wear long black socks in his casket.

As he walks the streets, still dusty from the protests that blocked his entry to the city days ago, he finds himself thinking: Is this an honor, granting his father his final wish, or is this his father's way of saying, *Get lost in this city you might have known?*

He's asked his half sisters if they know the socks' meaning, but they don't, and, judging by their faces, they don't care. The oldest of his half sisters says she stopped asking questions about his father a long time ago.

When Theo finally finds the socks in a small store about a mile from his father's apartment, they're thin, almost transparent. He pictures slipping them onto his father's feet and feels a rush of despair.

He makes his way to the front of the cluttered store, where a woman who looks to be his own age, thirtysomething, sits behind the counter smoking a cigarette. The shop is quiet. There's only one other patron in the store, a woman picking through a box of beauty products.

"How much?" Theo asks.

The woman hears Theo's accent and smiles. "What a time to come to China," she says. Only days later will Theo learn that the wreckage he witnessed on his way into the city came from the Tiananmen Square Massacre.


One day when Theo was eleven, his father, who people sometimes thought was his grandfather, picked him up from school and told him they were going to visit his half sister, who had just given birth. But when they got to the gate, he revealed his true plan: they were going to China.

His father was moving back to work for the Communists. They had agreed to give him the penthouse suite in the Beijing Hotel. Theo would be the coolest kid in school, get all the ladies. As a former high-ranking diplomat for the Nationalist government, his father would be celebrated as a man who'd seen the light.

Theo asked where his mother was, and his father explained that she didn't know about the plan yet, but once they got to China, she would have to join them, because once you got into China, there was no getting out. For years, he'd been trying to make her understand the necessity of this move, but she'd been stubborn, so now he was taking matters into his own hands.

Theo passed out on the plane—that was also what he did when his parents fought—and slept through the entire flight. When he woke up in Paris, it was to an officer locking his father's wrists into handcuffs and escorting his father into an interrogation room as another officer took Theo to a separate room down the hall. A man asked Theo questions and he provided the correct responses, something he was good at. ("What time did your father pick you up yesterday?" "It was right before lunch, so it must have been eleven fifteen." "When did you realize you weren't going to Michigan?" "When the gate said 'Paris.'")

In the middle of the questioning, another man came in to interrupt. Then the two men left, and minutes later, the new man returned and told Theo his mother was on her way to meet them. She was giving him a choice: he could go to China with his father, or return to Connecticut with her, but there was no way she was going to China and no way his father could return to the States.

In the meantime, in a rare act of lenience on her part, or perhaps strategy, she had decided to let Theo and his father spend the day in Paris. She would meet them at the airport the next morning.

They stopped first at a hotel, where they checked into a room with a king-size bed and a balcony overlooking a street full of restaurants and cafés.

From the balcony, Theo watched a man light a cigarette. It looked like he was waiting for someone inside, but when he finished smoking, he simply put out the cigarette and walked off. Nothing was as it seemed.

Theo sat at the desk in the hotel room while his father changed his clothes and listed the things they would do in Paris: visit the Louvre, the Eiffel Tower, go out for a nice meal. His father wore a knitted vest over a collared shirt with a tie, a blazer, a pair of black pants, and the cheap white sneakers his mother didn't like.

Theo wondered if he should also change his clothes. He was still wearing his school uniform. He hadn't showered. His father set out a plaid shirt, a pair of pants, and clean underwear, which Theo was thankful for. When Theo had finished getting dressed, his father took out his Polaroid and asked him to pose on the balcony. When Theo made a straight face for the camera, his father told him to smile.

At the Louvre, his father had one of his temper tantrums.

"I just saw you sell a ticket to another man!" he shouted, when the ticketer told him the museum was sold out for the hour.

"That was for a different gallery."

"Is this because I'm Chinese?"

"No, sir."

"My son and I are in Paris for one day. I'm not leaving this museum without seeing the *Mona Lisa*."

"You can come back in an hour."

"We don't have an hour." Theo felt everyone's eyes on them. He looked at the ground.

"I'd like to speak to your manager. I know you don't know who I am, but the last time I was in Paris, I was the secretary of the Chinese embassy in London. I was China's ambassador to Iran and Thailand. My son and I have twenty-four hours in Paris."

Five minutes later, his father put his arm around his shoulder as they took in the most famous painting in the world. "Everyone sees a different expression when they look at her," his father said. "What do you see?"

Theo stared and stared, but he could not understand or find language for her expression.

"I think she's cheering us on," said his father.

After the Louvre, they went to the Eiffel Tower and took the elevator to the top. When they stepped out onto the observation deck, Theo felt short of breath. From this height, everything looked fake, like a LEGO town. "This is what we'll be a part of in China," his father said. "The modernization of our nation. The return of China to the status of a world power."

Theo shot his father in the eye in his mind. He always shot his father after his father shot him. That was how they played cowboys and Indians. He'd lie there, dead, and his father would approach him to make sure it was over, and Theo would sit up and shoot his father in the eye. His father would stumble backward, covering his eye with his hand. He was the largest Chinese person Theo had ever seen, six feet tall, two hundred pounds. His mother would yell at them to come inside. They'd laugh. They'd feel stupid. Theo would stagger over to his father and fall. They'd lie there in the grass, on this planet suspended in air. What if Theo fell off the earth? He'd grab his father, roll onto his chest, and stay there.

Theo thought about their life in Connecticut. He knew his father wanted a job at Harvard or Columbia or Yale and felt let down by his job at the University of Hartford. He also knew his father no longer slept in the same bed as his mother. He knew his father was important in China and wanted to be important again. But wasn't their life enough? Their brown split-level and their new Chevy and their summer vacations? His mother worked at Bank of America. His parents hosted dinners for the Chinese American Student Association. He and his father played outside in the yard. At night it was so quiet all you could hear were the crickets. His father told him they were a sign of good luck.

After the Eiffel Tower, they went back to the hotel to get ready for dinner. His father had brought Theo's suit, but when Theo put it on, his father grimaced. "It's wrinkled," he said, and began looking around the room for an iron. When he found one, he studied it as if it were a strange object from an archaeological dig. "Do you put water in it?"

Theo shrugged.

His father picked up the phone and called the front desk. A few minutes later a woman arrived. "Bonjour," she said, when Theo's father opened the door. "Can I help you?"

Theo's father used his broken French to explain his needs to the woman. Her eyes opened wide when he spoke, then twinkled into an amused smile as she looked at Theo and then back at his father. She unfolded the ironing board and plugged in the iron. She had long blond hair twisted into a knot on top of her head and wore dark lipstick. When the iron was hot, she said something in French to Theo's father, and he handed her money. She started to iron Theo's suit. Afterward, Theo's father asked if she could iron his suit and offered her another bill, which she refused. By then, she and Theo's father were so engaged in conversation that they were laughing. Theo's father looked happier than Theo had seen him all day.

"Enchantée," the woman said to both of them, her cheeks flushed, before she left.


The restaurant was on the top floor of a hotel. Again, they had a view of the city. Theo's father was jittery with excitement about his steak. Theo heard his mother's voice in his head: *Steak only upsets your ulcers.* But his mother wasn't here. His father ordered a filet mignon and a glass of wine.

"The penthouse suite will have views like this restaurant," his father said. "Big windows overlooking the city. And we'll have a maid. You'll never need to make your bed again. We'll have a cook too. Your mother will never complain again about having to make us a meal."

Theo thought of the life his father used to live. He'd had a mansion for his eight children. Each child had their own room and their own nanny. In the dining room, the children's meals were served and their plates cleared. Theo's father was still an ambassador when the Revolution arrived. He fled with Theo's mother and left those eight children behind.

His first wife, whom he'd married in an arranged marriage, was able to get half the children out of China, but the other four got stuck. Theo's father got letters from them sometimes, claiming they were "honored to serve the motherland," but Theo's mother said not to trust anything coming from a government with censorship. According to the news in the United States, everyone in the reeducation programs worked fourteen-hour days in the fields without enough to eat.

His parents argued about this sometimes. His father asked why it was so hard for his mother to imagine that they could be both physically uncomfortable and spiritually nourished. They could be a part of something bigger than themselves.

"What if they send us to work camps?" Theo asked.

He saw the glint of fear in his father's eyes. "They won't."

"How do you know?"

"Trust me." Irritation had edged into his father's voice, and Theo, afraid of another scene like the one earlier, changed the subject. "Did you meet Mom in China?"

His father's mood lifted. He loved the past. "No," he said. "Your mother was my translator in Bangkok. Her parents were Chinese, but they lived in Thailand, so she grew up speaking both languages. I always thought she was so beautiful and mysterious. So one day I went up to her at a party and asked her to dance with me. She said, 'I like to keep two feet on the ground.' So I said, 'Stand there and I'll dance around you.' And I pranced around her, and I made her laugh, and the rest was history."

Theo could imagine this. His father's childish charm, his mother's tight smile giving way to him.

For the rest of the meal, they didn't discuss Theo's decision. Theo listened to his father talk to him about all the relatives waiting for them in China.

He knew most of this, but it was easier to listen than to speak, so he listened.

From where he sat now, looking out the window at the street, he heard his father get out of bed and run into the bathroom. The door slammed. Cue the sound of retching. He was paying for the steak. Theo saw his mother roll her eyes. He hated the sound, so he went out onto the balcony. The sharp cold felt good. He watched the people in the shadows. There were still some lights on in the restaurants.

He considered his choice again. Connecticut was boring, but China was dangerous. He'd seen the corpses in wheelbarrows on TV.

"My health will be better in China," his father said, coming out behind him. He put a hand on Theo's shoulder and told him to come inside. Theo followed.

Theo got into the bed far away from his father. He lay on his back while his father propped himself up on an elbow and faced him. "So," he said. "Have you made up your mind?"

Theo had an idea then, a revelation, cutting through him like lightning. He'd let his dreams decide for him. Wherever his dream took place, that's where he'd go. If his dream took place in the States, he'd stay in the States, and if his dream took place in China, he'd go to China.

"I'm going to go where my dream takes place," he said.

His father was quiet. Then he snorted. "You can't leave such an important decision to your dreams," he said.

It was his father's fault he had to make this horrible choice. His father didn't say anything more. He knew anything else he said could backfire.

Theo got up to brush his teeth. He studied himself in the mirror. Is this why his father had taken so many pictures of him today? To remember his face? Would he send them to his mother if Theo went to live with his father? He realized he hadn't been counting and started to count to sixty. He'd had a cavity that year, and his mother had told him he had to be careful to brush twice a day for sixty seconds or his teeth could fall out.

After he rinsed and spit and got back into bed, he found his left foot drifting closer to his father. His toes brushed against his father's leg. He liked the way it felt. He kept them there. He couldn't sleep, though, and neither could his father. Theo knew his father was awake, because when he slept, he snored so loudly it could wake the neighbors. Eventually, his father started to toss and turn. Theo moved away from him. He was afraid to inch closer to him, but he wanted to—wanted to grab him and roll on top of him like he used to. His father tossed and turned. It was a dance. A couple of times they opened their eyes at the same time and looked at each other.

In the morning, Theo startled awake and a dream barreled back to him, narrowed into focus. He was in their garage, lying on the ground. The door opened and his mother came out in a nightgown. "What are you doing in here?" she said. There were empty soda bottles strewn all around him. He had drunk all the soda and he was about to get in trouble for it. He was in West Hartford, Connecticut.

His father was out on the balcony when Theo woke up, thinking. He scared Theo when he was lost in thought, but Theo knew he took after his father in this way. His father had only one other son, from his first marriage. His half brother had visited once and given Theo caramels. He was one of the ones who had made it to the States. He had a big belly and a loud laugh. He was a travel agent.

Theo considered falling back asleep, but his father turned around and saw him too soon. He came over to Theo, who already had a scratch in his throat.

Theo didn't need to say anything. "I think she'll come around," his father said. "Once I'm there, she'll see. You two will both come live with me. The Communists are so happy that I'm returning, they'll do anything. They can arrange for you to come."

He truly believed this, and that is what set Theo over the edge. He cried and cried as his father told him everything was going to be all right. But it wouldn't be. Theo already knew this.


At the funeral, a number of Party officials have requested to speak after the family. One is a very beautiful woman whose long black hair is streaked with gray. "I was his friend during the hardest part of the Revolution," she says. "He was so eager to shed his bourgeois attitudes and embrace the hard work of the proletariat." "He was a dear friend and respected colleague," says another man, whom Theo does not trust, speaking of his father's time at the College of Foreign Affairs. The man doesn't mention that the college was really a holding cell for intellectuals during his time there; that of his father's fifty-two colleagues, fifty either disappeared or died from suicide. Theo learned this when his father came back to the States in 1972, following Nixon's reopening of relations with China, thin and humbled, looking for another professorship. "An indispensable comrade," says another man, who claims to have worked with his father recently, although Theo knows his father had not really worked in years—that after failing to find a job in the Unites States, he lived a quiet life in Beijing, researching and writing, mostly for his own eyes.

Then it is time for everyone to pay their respects at the casket. As people stop in front of his father, Theo notices the woman who spoke earlier staring at his father's feet.

"Are you looking at the socks?" Theo asks.

The woman glances around to make sure no one is watching, then motions for him to follow her outside.

When they're alone, she seems overly curious about him. "What do you do now?" she asks.

Theo can see that the woman knows about him—likely, even, about that day in Paris. He tells her about himself. He went to medical school at Columbia. He's a family doctor. His wife is a nurse. They just had their first child. He's lived in New York for almost a decade now.

"But what about the socks?" he asks again, worried that any moment someone with a red armband will interrupt them.

"We wore them inside our rubber boots," she says. "They were camp code. They protected our ankles from the leeches in the muddy fields. And even inside our rubber boots, they were always wet. One day, when he was taking them off, he said he would wear them in his casket. I thought he was kidding."

She puts her hand on his shoulder; there's a look of a regret in her eyes. "They're a symbol of his sacrifice," she says.

# INHERITANCE

*by* LAURA VAN DEN BERG

THE WOMAN HAD INHERITED the house from her stepfather, or the man she had come to think of as her stepfather. He and her mother had never legally wed, because by then her mother had been married and divorced three times and had decided enough was enough. Still, her mother and her stepfather had met when the woman was sixteen, and they had stayed together, in relative happiness, until her mother perished in a car accident. This happened just before the woman's thirtieth birthday, and she could still remember the gasping sound her stepfather had made when he called from the hospital. The woman had been aware that her stepfather owned a house in western Mexico, in a town popular with American and Canadian expats and as a weekend getaway for residents of Guadalajara. Neither the woman nor her mother had ever gone to the house, however, as it was rented out year-round. But a few years after her mother died, her stepfather stopped renting the house and moved there. He texted photos on occasion. The town sat on the shores of an enormous lake. There was a scenic Malecón, cobblestone streets, various plazas. Low blue mountains. The woman and her stepfather spoke on the phone two or three times a year, always on her birthday and on Christmas, but did not otherwise keep in touch.

So the call from her stepfather's lawyer—first, to tell her that her stepfather had died, and second, to tell her that he had left her the house—had come as quite a shock.

There were, the lawyer explained, some complications. In order to assume legal possession of the house—to keep it or sell it or simply take over the utility bills—the woman needed to acquire a permanent visa. In order to acquire a permanent visa, she would have to reside in the home for some period of time. He could help her with all the other steps, and the paperwork, but the residency point was, from the government's perspective, nonnegotiable.

"How long would I need to stay?" the woman asked. She worked remotely as an illustrator of instruction manuals. Seventeen illustrations for assembling a bookshelf. Six illustrations for installing a car seat.

"The process will take somewhere between three weeks and three months," the lawyer replied.

"Three *months?*"

"Unlikely," the lawyer admitted. "But not impossible."

Before the call ended, the woman asked if her stepfather had died of the fever, as she had assumed. This illness that had arrived out of nowhere and seemed determined to stick around. For five years, all of humanity had been sloshing about in the same turbulent sea. At times, the waves would flatten and the water would turn clear, and you couldn't blame a person for thinking the storm had passed. Then the waves reared back up and came crashing over heads.

"Oh, no," the lawyer replied. "Your stepfather died of a stroke. It happened in his sleep. All very peaceful."

The woman lived in a high-rise apartment building in Washington, DC. After the call with the lawyer ended, she walked over to her living room window, which looked out onto a massive parking lot. That afternoon, the sky was a flat slate gray. She could not remember how exactly her stepfather had come to acquire the house in the first place, or his history with the town, but she did remember that the lake had three small islands. Her stepfather had texted her a photo of one of them, with a little explanation of its history. She even remembered, to her astonishment, the names of these islands.

The woman was forty-one, and it was often so strange to her, the things people remembered.

Isla de los Alacranes and Isla Mezcala and Isla Menor.


The woman had imagined a small white adobe bungalow, based largely on photos she'd seen in travel magazines, but that was not what she found when the taxi dropped her at the address. The property took up an entire block and was surrounded by tall terra-cotta walls with bright pink bougainvillea spilling over the edges. She stood at the front door—rounded at the top and made from wood that had been stained a rich, coppery brown—no longer sure if *house* was the right word. Perhaps she should be calling the property a villa or a compound. She rapped the lion's head door knocker and waited.

The lawyer opened the front door. His name was Òscar Bonifacio, and he was older than he had sounded on the phone, perhaps sixty. She could tell from the silver in his eyebrows and in his hair, which had been combed back. He wore a dark, well-cut suit and black oxfords and a white N95 that turned his profile beakish. They all looked like large, confused birds in these masks, the woman had thought as she waded through the airport. She followed Òscar Bonifacio up a short flight of stairs and through a small tiled mezzanine, with plants in glazed pots and a hammock, and into a spacious living room. Just beyond the living room there was a galley kitchen with blue tile counters, and beyond that, through the tall windows, she could see a yard and, she thought, the glimmering edge of a swimming pool.

"It's quite a place, isn't it?" Òscar Bonifacio sat down in a royal blue armchair and crossed his legs. He steepled his hands on his knee.

The woman sat across from him on a pale pink divan. She sat very straight and on the edge, like a child afraid to make a mess. She felt confused—her understanding of her stepfather was being reorganized in real time—and overwhelmed by the scope and scale of everything.

"To tell you the truth, I was expecting something more modest," she said.

In her understanding, her stepfather and mother had been comfortable, but not in excess. They had both been public high school teachers: her mother English, her stepfather biology. When her mother died, there had not been an inheritance, but there was ample money for funeral expenses—a blessing in this world. She'd had no idea her stepfather's property was so opulent, but it wasn't just that. Her stepfather had favored Teva sandals and North Face. He knew how to change a tire, clean a fish, put up gutters. He'd been the one to give her driving lessons, on country roads in coastal Maryland. He'd taught her to surf at Assateague and how to pry open oysters with a small, sharp knife. He had a sense of adventure, in other words, but he had also been practical.

"We knew each other for many years," Òscar Bonifacio said. He explained that her stepfather had first come here for the Carrerade Montaña la Chupinaya, a footrace to the summit of Cerro la Chupinaya and then back to the central plaza. Her stepfather had passed out before the finish line and had to be carried into town.

"It was the altitude," Òscar Bonifacio said. "You must be sure to drink plenty of water."

"Do you know how he came to own this house?" the woman asked. "I just... well, this place doesn't seem like him at all."

"He inherited the house from a friend," Òscar Bonifacio said. "A German fellow. One of the runners who helped carry him—over the years they became good friends. Very close. The only condition was that nothing about the décor or the furnishings could be changed. Maintained, of course, but not changed."

"That explains a lot," the woman said, looking around.

"I'm afraid that rule applies to you as well."

"Oh." It was hard for her to imagine how such a rule would be enforced, considering that the original owner and her stepfather were both dead.

Òscar Bonifacio clapped his hands and stood. "How about a tour?"

The house had three bedrooms and a balcony that overlooked the Malecón. In the backyard, there was an avocado tree—the fruits lay gleaming in the grass, large as bowling balls—and a saltwater swimming pool. The last thing Òscar Bonifacio pointed out was the casita, a small guesthouse with its own courtyard, connected to the tiled mezzanine by a freestanding spiral staircase.

"Large groups could rent the entire property," he explained, "or the casita could be rented on its own. To solo travelers, for the most part. People like you."

"People like me," the woman repeated. On the tour, she had been struck that she could not find a trace of her mother anywhere in the house—not a single photo or trinket.

"So what happens now?" the woman said once they were back at the front door.

"You wait for my call," said Òscar Bonifacio. "You get to know your inheritance. Have you ever had an inheritance before?"

"I have not." She felt a little embarrassed and a little proud to state this fact. She suspected Òscar Bonifacio was used to dealing with people who had inheritances galore.

"I'm of the mind that it's best for inheritances not to come too soon," he said. "The later they arrive, the more they are appreciated."

"Yes," the woman said. "I can see how that would be true."

She watched Òscar Bonifacio disappear around a corner before closing the heavy wood door. She hoped she hadn't appeared ungrateful—in fact, the opposite was true. She was stunned by her stepfather's magnanimity, especially considering that they were not related by blood. She was spinning. One minute she was illustrating a manual for hanging window blinds and the next she was in a grand house in another country, awaiting a permanent visa. By that point in her life, she had become an Instacart devotee and left her building only when the cases receded, for errands, and for the occasional coffee with a friend. She never had guests, and she kept her apartment sparsely furnished. She told herself that she was happy in the safety of her little cave. How had her reality transformed so quickly? It seemed impossible.

That night, she lay down on each of the three beds, like the golden-haired girl in the children's story, before picking the one closest to the living room. That was the only one where she could hear signs of life outside—musicians playing in the park by the Malecón, a car backfiring, voices drifting down the street.


The woman slept late. When she woke, there was a text from Òscar Bonifacio.

"There's been a surge in cases. Everything is shutting down. Best to stay indoors until circumstances improve."

The fever was not the first plague that had happened in the woman's lifetime. Throughout her thirties, she had been hired to illustrate countless manuals for how to wear a mask properly and how to thoroughly wash your hands and how to disinfect a contaminated space. The fever was not any more deadly than the others—just the most persistent. Now the waves were swelling again, getting ready to swallow up anyone who remained in their path.

She summoned the local news on her phone and read about the spike in cases. Already a nearby hospital was at capacity. It used to be that cases would steadily climb until they finally peaked and then retreated, only for the cycle to repeat in a few months, but now these surges came without warning. Like clear-day flooding. One minute you could go for a walk and visit a café and the next the hospitals were overflowing and no one could go anywhere. During the lulls, people could pretend the lives they'd once had might still be recovered, but it was only a matter of time before the truth asserted itself.

For the time being, however, the woman could go places without leaving the property. She put on her bathing suit and took a dip in the pool. She floated on her back and stared up at the large, fluffy clouds. They stayed perfectly still in the sky, as though they were part of a stage or a set. Afterward she put on an old oversize T-shirt, pulled out the front and gathered as many avocados as she could in the fabric. She found a large white bowl in the kitchen to store the avocados. The skins were rippled and deep green. Almost reptilian. She was hacking into one of them with a knife when she heard a strange clanging sound coming from the interior courtyard.

She went out onto the mezzanine and peered down into the private courtyard of the casita. Here, ivy climbed the walls instead of bougainvillea. The fluffy clouds had flown away and the sun was very bright. A cream shade sail made an angular shadow on the ground. An intruder in a straw hat was sitting in a rattan club chair, playing a triangle.

"Hello?" The woman's voice echoed slightly, as though she were speaking into a well. "What do you think you're doing here?"

The intruder stopped playing. She stood up from the chair and turned toward the mezzanine. She had long, pointed features and blond hair that looked permed. She was not wearing a mask and the woman felt a wave of panic move over her. Were they far enough away from each other? She pulled her T-shirt collar over her mouth.

"What happened to Seth?" The intruder pointed her silver percussion stick up at the woman.

Seth had been the name of her stepfather.

"Seth died," the woman said. "I'm his stepdaughter."

"Good riddance, if you don't mind me saying." The intruder had thin pink lips and ice-blue eyes.

"I do mind!" the woman shouted through her T-shirt.

"Let me tell you a little story about Seth. He moved back here and he kicked me out of the casita. Even though I had a month left on my rental. Well, I have since consulted my higher power and my higher self, and I have returned to claim the time that is owed to me."

She went back to striking the triangle with the percussion stick. Her wrist moved so quickly that it looked as if she were whipping egg whites.

The woman's stepfather had always been sensitive to noise and would not have appreciated all this clanging.

"You have to go," the woman called out, but the intruder was undeterred.

She rushed inside and texted Òscar Bonifacio. Did he know anything about her stepfather kicking out a woman who had a month left on her lease? Her bathing suit was still wet under her T-shirt and she was starting to feel chilled.

She took a hot shower and got dressed. She combed her wet hair back into a ponytail. She put on a mask and surgical gloves. She did not know where this intruder had been previously or what she might be carrying.

She took the spiral staircase down into the courtyard and knocked on the casita door. When the intruder answered, she was wearing a mask, to the woman's relief, and large black sunglasses, giving her a buggy aura. Also, she had changed into a red one-piece bathing suit, her torso covered by a white linen wrap.

"You're American, right?" She hoped it might help to find some common ground.

"Lyme, Connecticut," the intruder replied. "The plague capital of the nation."

"You don't want to go back home? Given everything?"

"Civil war has broken out in America," the intruder said. "Haven't you heard?"

"No, no," the woman said. She had just left America, the capital city, and there had been no civil war. Of course there had not. Still, the authority with which the intruder spoke made her feel a little woozy.

"Don't shoot the messenger." The intruder held up her palms.

"I'm sorry about what happened with my stepfather," the woman pressed on. "I'm sure we can figure out, well, some kind of financial solution. A way to get you what you're owed. But you can't stay here."

"This house is big enough for eight people," the intruder said. "At least. This town is in a state of emergency and you won't offer one person shelter? If I hadn't felt called to play my triangle, you would not even have known I was down here."

The woman stared at the floor. She felt her cheeks go hot. It was true that a cruel thing about plagues was the way they made people pull up their drawbridges and fortify their walls.

"Where did you go after my stepfather kicked you out?" the woman asked.

"I moved in with my lover," the intruder said. "But we broke up two days ago. You think this is a nice house? Well, let me tell you. He had a *great* house. If I knew there was going to be another surge, I might have toughed it out for a few more months." She paused and adjusted her sunglasses. "To tell you the truth, I am going through an emotional crisis. A romantic crisis. A midlife crisis. An existential crisis. To tell you the truth, I am, at the moment, extremely fragile."

The woman had never been good at dealing with other people's emotions. She had inherited this trait from her mother, who did not like to discuss difficult subjects. This was why the woman appreciated her line of work, which she got to undertake in solitude. When her illustrations included people, it was usually just one part—like a hand—and even when they included whole bodies, the faces were blank, free of feeling.

"Maybe you should just stay put for now," the woman said as she retreated into the courtyard.

In the kitchen, the knifed avocado was still on the counter. She googled "Has civil war broken out in America." The answer was, more or less, "not just yet." She heard splashing and saw the intruder in the pool, in a snorkel and goggles. She kept diving underwater and paddling around, like she was searching for exotic fish or treasure.

The woman ate three avocados for lunch, with a little olive oil and sea salt, and then sat out on the balcony. The sky was hard and bright as a shield. She could see the lake. The whole town seemed empty—the Malecón, the streets. On occasion, she saw a person in a mask, walking with a hunched urgency. Sirens came in waves, high and then low, high and then low. She was about to take a nap when she got a text from Òscar Bonifacio. The intruder's name was Freya Regina. She was indeed an American and she had indeed been living in the casita when her stepfather moved here permanently. They had become romantically involved and it had not ended well. That was why she'd been kicked out. Although Òscar Bonifacio did not use that language. Instead he said "excused from the residence." The woman texted back and asked Òscar Bonifacio what exactly he meant by "ended badly."

"Have you ever seen the movie *Fatal Attraction*?" he replied.

\*   \*   \*

The next day, the woman resolved to pretend that Freya Regina did not exist. This was how she preferred to deal with problems: to will them into absence. She had once ignored an ache in her molar for months. After the fever came, she persisted in ending emails with "Here's hoping all this will be over soon!" for three years straight. When it came to Freya Regina, she could not think of what else to do. For reasons of ethics and physical fitness, she could hardly drag her from the casita and toss her out onto the street.

She opened her email and started to review the instructions for her next illustration job. It was for a household contraption she had never heard of before. The assembled thing was shaped like a small white toaster oven. You could put items weighing less than a pound inside—a fork, for example, or an orange—and the contraption would produce a clone. It seemed like such an invention would be extremely helpful in addressing many problems, like food insecurity, except the product details revealed that it was very expensive. When exactly had this technology been invented, anyway? For a moment, the woman wondered if she had slept through some major developments in the world around her. Like most of her employers, the product manufacturers wanted the hands in the drawings to be small and colorless, with short oval fingernails. Only four illustrations to show how the contraption should be assembled. Far less than a piece of furniture.

In the afternoon, the woman was having a coffee on the balcony when she heard an alarming sound in the backyard. A series of minor detonations. She looked out the window. Freya Regina had gathered a bunch of avocados in a wicker laundry basket. The woman watched her pick up a gleaming green head, lurch back like a pitcher on a mound, and hurl the avocado against the wall. "Stop that," the woman called out, even though all the windows were closed. "Stop that right now!" Freya Regina persisted in hurling the avocados. Destructive and wasteful, the woman thought as she turned from the window. Her stepfather had disliked wastefulness. He had recycled and composted in the '80s. She could not imagine what he could have seen in Freya Regina.

In the afternoon, she was hard at work on an illustration for the cloning contraption when she got the strange feeling that someone, or something, was behind her. She turned around in her chair and Freya Regina was on the pink divan, paging through an architectural magazine. She wore a black mask attached to a crystal lanyard. Quite elegant, the woman had to admit.

"What's your opinion on brutalist architecture?" Freya Regina asked, turning a page.

"You're supposed to stay in the casita," the woman said. "What are you doing here?"

"The casita has become rather claustrophobic, I'm afraid."

The woman turned her chair around to face the sofa, but did not get any closer.

"I asked my stepfather's lawyer about you," the woman said. "He told me that you were in a relationship, a romantic relationship, with my stepfather."

"Òscar Bonifacio told you that Seth and I were lovers?" Freya Regina replied, sounding almost amused.

"It seems you have not been honest with me."

"Or Òscar has not been honest with *you*." She closed the magazine and slapped it down on the table. "He and Seth were lovers for years!"

"What?" the woman said. "No, that's not possible."

"Well, don't be all homophobic about it."

"I'm not homophobic," said the woman sharply.

It was just that each time her understanding of her stepfather was disturbed, it sent a ripple through the rest of her world. After the ripple passed, everything took on a slightly different shape, like a room that kept getting rearranged in minor ways.

"Terrible about that plane crash, isn't it?" Freya Regina said next.

The woman blinked. She felt a fuzziness at the edges of the living room, as though a light snow were falling somewhere just beyond her periphery.

"What plane crash?"

Freya Regina explained that a plane from a major American carrier had crashed in the mountains outside Durango three days ago. They were still recovering the bodies, still searching for the black box. Presumably it was a plane full of Americans, hoping to get across the border before they became causalities of the civil war.

"I had no idea," the woman said. "How awful."

"You must not be much for the news," Freya Regina said next. "What do you do for a living?"

"I illustrate instruction manuals."

"I hope you don't work for IKEA," she said.

"I've never worked for IKEA." The woman added that right now she was illustrating a manual for a new cloning device. She explained about the one-pound rule and how the contraption was supposed to work.

"If such a thing existed, we could have avocados year-round," Freya Regina said. "Imagine!"

"Well, it *does* exist. Or it will soon. Otherwise they'd have no need for a manual." The woman paused. "And what about you? How do you make your way in the world?"

"I am a woman of action," Freya Regina said.

"What kind of action?" asked the woman.

"A little too soon to say," replied Freya Regina.

\*   \*   \*

It turned out that Freya Regina was a chef. She was fluent in Spanish and had once worked for a high-end restaurant in Guadalajara known for molecular desserts. The high-end restaurant closed during the first year of the fever and after that she'd moved south to this town. The woman discovered all this a few days after their conversation in the living room. By then cases had dipped and people were starting to venture out. From the mezzanine, she had watched Freya Regina struggle into the courtyard, laden with cloth shopping bags filled with fine ingredients. The woman spotted fish or meat wrapped in brown paper, a large, pale wheel of cheese, verdant bundles of tatsoi, a bottle of wine. She smelled fresh bread. That evening, she peered over the railing again and saw Freya Regina eating a meal for one that looked like it had been teleported from a gourmet restaurant: fish cooked in parchment, green beans with almonds, golden fingerling potatoes. She had called down and asked Freya Regina where she'd learned to cook, and that's when the woman was told about the restaurant in Guadalajara where they shaped chocolate mousse into tiny skulls, which they then coated in edible gold.

There were other things the woman wanted to ask Freya Regina about. For starters, she had searched the news for a plane crash and had not been able to find anything concerning an American carrier (or any other major airline, for that matter). She wondered where Freya Regina was getting her news from. Perhaps she was one of those conspiracy theorists who got all her information from underground chat rooms. Nevertheless, the woman felt a little unsettled that her news results seemed to produce an entirely different reality than Freya Regina's.

The case counts continued to fall. The woman realized how pent-up she'd been feeling in the house. How much she had been longing to go outside and explore. Maybe she didn't want to live forever in a cave, after all. As soon as it was permissible, she booked a charter boat to Isla de los Alacranes. That was the one her stepfather had told her about; she remembered that the island had gotten its name because it was shaped like a scorpion. On the phone, the captain informed her that the price sheet started with two passengers—that is, the cost for one person would be no less than the cost for a pair. The captain kept asking for the name of the second passenger, and the woman kept trying to explain that it would be just her, and then the captain would again explain about the price, and eventually she said the second passenger was Freya Regina. She couldn't think of anyone else in the moment, and the name just burst out of her. At first, she assured herself that she was under no obligation to actually invite Freya Regina, but then she began to wonder if maybe it would be a good idea. Or *an* idea, anyway. Maybe they could start fresh, focus on their similarities. Two Americans in the same country. Two women alone. So she knocked on the casita door and asked Freya Regina if she'd like to join her.

"The lake can still be crossed?" Freya Regina said. "I thought Guadalajara had sucked it dry by now." She was wearing a baby blue apron over her red bathing suit. Something terrifically fragrant wafted over from the small kitchen. Butter and onions. Perhaps the start of a sauce.

"Apparently it can," said the woman.

In the morning, they walked over to the dock and boarded a small white yacht. Only twenty minutes to reach the island. Freya Regina rode in the bridge, to keep out of the wind, but the woman stayed on the stern side. She watched the town shrink and the lake grow larger. The frothing wake followed like the tail of a creature.

The night before, she'd read that the lake had lost half its depth. When she looked over the railing, she could, at times, see to the bottom. The small, swaying clusters of aquatic plants. In recent years, the lake had become a dead zone for marine life, as factories upstream funneled more and more pollution into the water.

Once they had docked, the captain took out a map and pointed to a few attractions. He and Freya Regina talked easily together in Spanish, laughing like old friends. Freya Regina explained that there was a restaurant, a lighthouse, a chapel. She suggested they stop at the restaurant for cazuelas, a mix of juices and tequila, served with fruit skewers. The restaurant was run by a young couple. They were the only other people the woman had seen on the island. Was it not safe to go out, after all? Had they made a mistake by coming here?

"Did you know that my stepfather inherited the house from a friend?" the woman asked Freya Regina. They were sitting under an umbrella, nibbling on their fruit skewers. "Kind of unusual, don't you think?"

"Oh yes! Franco. One summer, he saved Seth from drowning. After that, they became close friends."

The woman was certain that Òscar Bonifacio had told her that the friend had come to her stepfather's aid during a road race. Yet another small misalignment.

"Well, however they met, leaving him that house was a very generous gift."

"An inheritance is not exactly a gift." Freya Regina sat a little taller in her chair. She was wearing the same straw hat as she had been on the day they met. "More like a responsibility. You become the custodian of something larger than yourself."

"A responsibility," the woman repeated, feeling uncertain, as she usually did, about Freya Regina's interpretation of things.

They followed a stone path past tan satellite dishes and white egrets plucking insects from the soil and a dog-sized scorpion carved out of gray rock. They found a small chapel with turquoise walls and a fresco of the Virgin Mary inside, hovering over a body of water, violet mountains as a backdrop. Underneath the Virgin Mary was a large gold scorpion with open claws. Painted on the scorpion's body was the island, a scattering of small structures and squat green trees. The woman tried to remember the biblical significance of scorpions. When she was a child, her mother had taught Sunday school, though the woman had paid only halfhearted attention to the stories. She remembered a passage about someone asking for an egg and getting a scorpion instead, but was unable to recall the larger context.

The woman was back on the stone path, walking uphill in the direction of the lighthouse, when she realized that Freya Regina was no longer behind her. She was alone, surrounded by green foliage. She backtracked down to the chapel, but there was still no sign of Freya Regina. Had she gone ahead to the lighthouse? The woman walked briskly up the small hill to the white lighthouse, which seemed to stand at a slight tilt, but still she could not find her traveling companion.

She stared up at the cloudless sky. Something about the blue blankness made her heart beat faster. A sweat broke out on her palms. She told herself that Freya Regina had just gone back down to the restaurant for another cazuela, or to the dock, but she could not find her at either of those places. The couple had not seen her, nor had the captain.

The captain turned out to be from Labrador, though he had lived in this town for thirty years. He offered to help her look for Freya Regina. Together they began combing the paths and the bushes as if they were searching for a lost wallet or a piece of jewelry. They went back to the chapel and to the lighthouse. After several hours, they had circled the small island many times. At that point, the only thing the woman could think was that Freya Regina had gotten the idea to go for a swim and something had happened. She had hit her head. She had drowned.

The woman felt a cracking in her chest, a sharp and sudden reminder of why she had always found comfort in a simple and solitary life. She was much less vulnerable to loss, hidden away in the cave.

Finally, there was nothing more to do but return to the mainland. The woman left her phone number with the couple, in the event that Freya Regina turned up. When she got back to the house, she would call the authorities and report that Freya Regina had gone missing on the island.

On the return, the lake was choppy. The woman asked the captain if she could use the bathroom and he directed her down a short, steep flight of stairs. At the bottom there was a small study—a desk lit by a single lamp—and then the door to the bathroom. On the desk, a gold compass sat on a paper map. The edges of the map were held down by lovely glass millefiori paperweights. Also, there was a familiar-looking instrument, boxy and white. The woman picked up the instrument and turned it over. It was the cloning contraption that she had been writing the instruction manual for. She ran a fingertip over the company name etched on the bottom. She put the instrument down and opened the desk drawer, moving with breathless certainty. She rifled through the drawer until she located a small manual. In the moment, she felt as though she were being guided by a future version of herself. She opened the manual and began turning the pages. The directions were in Spanish, but right away she recognized her own illustrations. The anonymous hand. The two buttons on the side of the machine, one square and one round. How could this be? She was looking for something to test the contraption with when the yacht slowed—they were approaching the harbor—and the captain called down the stairs, asking if she was all right.

When the woman returned to her stepfather's house, the wood door was unlocked. From the mezzanine, she could hear voices inside. In the living room, she found Òscar Bonifacio sitting on the pink divan, swirling a golden liquid around in a tumbler, and Freya Regina in the kitchen. She wore the same baby blue apron over a simple black dress, her blond hair pulled back into a long, frizzy braid. A third person was there, standing by the balcony doors and looking out at the lake. The woman could tell she was older, even before she turned around, from her silvered chignon. She wore an emerald green skirt suit, stockings, and slim black heels.

The woman was in khaki shorts and a white T-shirt, the armpits ringed with sweat. She felt ashamed of her appearance, despite being in the house that she had inherited, surrounded by people she had not invited over for dinner. And, in the case of the older woman, that she did not even know.

"You made it," Òscar Bonifacio said, rising from the sofa. There was a light surprise in his voice, as if her return had been an open question. "Let me get you a glass of wine."

She followed him to the kitchen, where Freya Regina was overseeing a symphony of trembling silver pots and crackling pans. She had been under the impression that Freya Regina and Òscar Bonifacio did not particularly care for each other, but on that evening they appeared to be thick as thieves.

"What happened," the woman said. She felt her fingers open and close around the cool stem of a wineglass. "On the island. Where did you go? We were hysterical. We looked everywhere."

"I had to get back." Freya Regina lifted a pot lid and began stirring the contents furiously with a wooden spoon. "We're having a dinner party. Can't you see?"

"I thought you had drowned!"

"Drowned? Not likely. I was a competitive swimmer in college."

When she turned toward the living room, the older woman was standing so close that she jumped back a little, sloshing the wine in her glass.

"I was a friend of your stepfather's. I live two blocks down. On Ocampo. We were neighbors, you see." She extended a warm, dry hand. She had a tattoo of a pomegranate—ripe to bursting—on the inside of her wrist. In the months after her mother's death, the woman had had a recurring dream about pomegranates. In the dream, she would open a suitcase and find that it was full of them. She still thought it very strange that there was not a single trace of her mother anywhere in this house.

The woman took a sip of wine and felt the velvet heat slide into her body.

"Has there been any progress on the permanent visa?" she asked Òscar Bonifacio. It seemed more and more urgent to get out of here as quickly as she could. Put the house on the market from a safe distance. Go back to her life in the DC high-rise. To the cave. She told herself that she could reject Freya Regina's perspective. That she did not have to become the custodian of anything.

"I'm afraid not." He smiled like he was giving her good news. "But that's to be expected at this stage. You've only been here for a week, after all."

Just before dinner was ready, Òscar Bonifacio pushed on a blank part of the living room wall and a door swung open. The woman gasped.

"Oh dear," he said. "Did I forget to show you the dining room?"

The woman crept toward the room and peered inside. There was a long wood table, set with plates and flatware and white candles, the wicks not yet lit. Four dining chairs, one at each head and two across from each other. They looked heraldic, made of ornately carved wood and wine-colored velvet, with little lions' heads for feet.

"Where did all this come from?" the woman asked as Òscar Bonifacio lit the candles.

"I'm an antiques dealer." The neighbor rested a thin hand on the woman's shoulder. "The man your stepfather inherited the house from had a wonderful eye."

A few minutes later, Freya Regina emerged from the kitchen carrying plates, one in each hand and the other two balanced on her forearms. A true professional. Freya Regina and Òscar Bonifacio took the chairs at the heads of the table; the woman and the neighbor sat across from each other. On each plate was a marbled puddle of boeuf bourguignon, tucked inside a velvety ring of mashed potatoes. Freya Regina took the first bite, chewing slowly with her eyes closed.

"Here's to being out and about again," Òscar Bonifacio said, raising his glass.

"Speak for yourself," said the neighbor. "I've *been* out and about."

She explained that she belonged to a virtual community of Canadian expats, who gathered in a replica of a village in Nova Scotia, much like the one she had grown up in.

"I grow lilacs year-round in my garden," the neighbor continued. "The metaverse is going to save us all from going mad in our own homes." She paused. "But someone wants to buy the village. A developer. We're going to have to band together and protest. To resist. Maybe pool our resources and buy the village ourselves, as a collective." She spoke as though this were all happening in real life.

"I'm not much for the metaverse myself," said Òscar Bonifacio. "I prefer to stay in the here and now."

The woman did not have strong feelings about the metaverse. The tangible world seemed, at the moment, like more than enough. She felt a little lightheaded, perhaps from being outdoors for so long. She wished there were water at the table, but there was only wine, and somehow she did not feel she could ask for water, even though she was dining in the house she had recently inherited.

"So which one of you was fucking my stepfather?" The woman put her fork down and looked around the table.

"Not I," said the neighbor. "My fucking days are well behind me."

"It doesn't have to be that way, you know." Freya Regina looked at the neighbor with sympathy.

"Your stepfather was a man of varied interests." Òscar Bonifacio raised his glass and swirled the wine around, as though he meant to make another toast.

The woman sank deeper into her large chair. Ever since her arrival, she had felt like she was attempting to scale a flat, slick rock face. No matter what she did, she could not find purchase.

"I am so sorry," the neighbor said, "about what is happening in your country. You must be absolutely beside yourself."

"It hasn't happened yet," the woman said quietly. She stared down into her lap.

After they finished dinner, Freya Regina cleared the plates and brought out an enormous trifle in a cut-crystal bowl. The dessert did not have three or four layers, like the other trifles the woman had seen. This one had at least a dozen, possibly more. Cream, sponge cake, jelly, various types of fruit. Òscar Bonifacio brought out four vintage sherry glasses and opened a bottle of port.

The woman had struggled to finish her boeuf bourguignon—each forkful had felt like jamming more clothes into a suitcase that could barely zip—but she could not stop eating the dessert.

Over the port and the trifle, Freya Regina brought up the plane crash again. She said that the rescue operation had found the black box.

"Flight number nineteen twelve. A very unlucky number for travel. Nineteen twelve was the year the *Titanic* hit that iceberg. I would never board a flight with such a number myself."

The woman felt her breath catch. The flight she had taken from DC to Guadalajara had been 1912. The number had stuck in her mind for some reason. Perhaps because of the *Titanic*.

"Where did the flight leave from?" the woman asked. She tried to focus on the flavor of sugar and cream on her tongue. She told herself that life was full of strange and inexplicable coincidences.

"Somewhere on the East Coast," Òscar Bonifacio said. "Isn't that right?"

"It was Dulles," said Freya Regina, who had evidently been following this situation quite closely. She radiated grave elegance, sitting at the head of the table in her black dress. "The plane left from Dulles."

The woman put her fork down. She stared at what remained of the trifle in the cut-crystal bowl, all those layers collapsing into one another.

"But my flight left from Dulles." Her voice was hoarse. "And the number was nineteen twelve. I'm sure of it."

"But if you think about it, hundreds of flights leave from Dulles every single day." Òscar Bonifacio leaned forward in his chair, looking thoughtful. "Surely they must recycle the numbers."

"And you're right here with us." The neighbor reached across the table, even though the woman's hand was well out of reach. "Thank goodness."

"Yes," the woman said, glancing at the faces of her dining companions. All three of them looked a little golden, as if they were being bathed in light emanating from a source she could not see. "So I am."

"This flight was shot down before it could make it out of America," Freya Regina continued. "That's what the authorities are saying, based on what was recovered from the black box. I think you'd remember if your flight had been shot down."

"Shot down by who?" the woman asked. The same clammy feeling that she'd experienced on the island made its return, descending over her like a thick fog.

"That has yet to be determined," said Freya Regina.

"Nothing bad ever happens in the metaverse," the neighbor said. "At least not yet. That's why I like it there."

The woman tried to recall the last time she felt she had arrived in a place where nothing bad could happen to her. She remembered a tree she used to climb in the woods behind her childhood home in Maryland. A horse chestnut, with large, sturdy branches that smelled like fresh straw. Yes. Maybe that had been the place.

After they were finished, the woman rose from her chair and began carrying plates into the kitchen. She moved without thinking, as though in a trance. She rinsed the plates. The warm water felt good on her hands. She left the glasses on the tile counter. She could get to those in the morning. When she looked up, her three guests—or was she their guest?—had gathered on the balcony. Òscar Bonifacio and Freya Regina were sharing a cigarette. They all appeared to be looking at something outside.

The woman went out into the backyard. The outdoor lights were off. She could see the tiny stars glistening behind smoky clouds. The trees along the wall were blanketed in shadow. In the center, the pool looked luminous, enticing. She took off her shorts and slipped into the water in her soiled T-shirt and underwear. She paddled around in loose circles. She dunked her head several times, as if she were trying to wake herself from a long, strange dream.

She looked up and caught a plane crossing the midnight sky. The blinking lights cut through gauzy clouds. The plane was, of course, too distant for her to discern anything about where it had come from or whom it might be carrying. She wished she could watch the plane descend onto the runway. Just to be assured that things still worked in the way she imagined they did. The sky rippled once, twice, like a sheet on a clothesline in a high wind. The woman stood upright in the pool, sloshing the water around. She thought she could feel Freya

Regina and Òscar Bonifacio and the neighbor watching her from the kitchen, but when she looked toward the house, no one was there. What had just happened? Was this the end? The sky went still, but it was not the same sky as it had been before. This one was starless. Free of flight.

# UNDOCUMENTED MEMORIES

*by* ANDREA BAJANI

*translated by Elizabeth Harris*

I.

WE'VE DOCUMENTED OUR SON'S entire story so far—two and a half years since his birth—with around twenty cell phone photos a day, except for several days in January 2020, from the twenty-second to the twenty-sixth. The last photo on January 22 shows our son in his stroller, reading, if you could call it that, a cloth-bound book. There are three identical photos, all taken moments apart. The evidence suggests he was posed just long enough to get the shot. He isn't even five months old, unable to turn the pages, but these are his first photos as a reader.

Somewhere between January 22 and 26, in 2020, we rushed our son to the Texas Children's Hospital in Houston because he had a seizure on the drive home from a quick meal at the House of Pies on Kirby Drive. He'd cried inconsolably in the parking lot while we tried in vain to calm him, and then he lost consciousness in the car. I was driving, my wife was sitting next to him in the back.

What I know about those moments after dinner comes from what my wife reported and the glimpses of her face I saw in the rearview mirror as she kept repeating our son's name, ever more breathlessly, leaning over him. I kept asking her to tell me what was going on back there, and at a certain point she caught my eye and said, "We need to go to the hospital." Our son was quiet, my wife was trying to bring him back by calling his name, and finally she handed me the phone with a voice—the GPS lady's voice—giving me directions to the emergency room. In the emergency room, and in the days that followed, when the doctors asked what had happened, my wife repeated the same version of the facts over and over, dozens of times. The baby was suddenly, convulsively crying, not like his normal crying, he lost consciousness in the car, he stopped responding to her, then his head jerked a few times, then nothing.

The last memory I have of our son before he went into the hospital—he was brought there at once from a nearby ER—is of him in his car seat, being strapped into the ambulance. He's awake now, and they've drawn blood. It's ten at night, and beside him, my wife is confirming—before she'll let the ambulance go—that the hospital we're headed to is in-network. I'm sitting in the car, motor on, a short distance back.

A few minutes later, my wife waves to me, indicating that we can go. She climbs into the ambulance, and a paramedic closes the door, gets in front. We leave, me following close behind. No sirens, moderate speed. My wife texts me as I drive. "If we get separated," she writes, "here's the hospital's address." I plug it into the GPS, let my navigator—who speaks Italian—be my guide. I don't think about anything; I drive, my eyes fixed on the ambulance. I speed up when they speed up, slow down when they slow down. I'm afraid of yellow lights, but if the ambulance goes through, so do I. The woman's voice on the phone, mispronouncing all the streets, is soothing, my one companion in my own language. These are the first two weeks of my American life.

## 2.

Even now, I don't know the exact day our son was hospitalized for a seizure. I could ask my wife, and more than likely she could pull up the date. But it's not an episode we care to discuss. We avoid it if we can, like it never happened. Sometimes it does come up, but purely for factual reasons—streets, stores—and once it appears, it soon fades away again. More than likely, my wife does remember the date, the day at the end of January when all this happened. I don't think she'd need to figure it out via photographs, like I would, but almost certainly there's a gap on her phone, too, from Wednesday, January 22, to Sunday, January 26, 2020.

One thing is certain: he was in the hospital for twenty-four hours; we spent the night in his assigned room. But now that I'm writing this, I'm suddenly not sure if it was one night or two. Again: I could go ask my wife, but she's only just woken up, and I don't want to force her to start her day with this. It's 5:00 a.m., our son's asleep in his room, watched over by a Snoopy in his airplane painted on the wall over his bed. These early hours in the morning we devote to correspondence, to writing, or to silence, coffee, and reading the paper. When he wakes up, everything is a race, there's no time for anything, everything's an emergency, more or less cheerful, depending on what he's dreamed, and ends when I drop him off at day care and he blows me a kiss before the teacher closes the door and he races up the one step to the sink to wash his hands by 8:00.

He might have been hospitalized for twenty-four or forty-eight hours, but the lack of documentation is a longer period than the time he spent in the hospital. There are no photos of the hospital, the building, the hallways, his room, or the luxurious play area on the ward. Or of the return home. The first photo on January 26 isn't a picture—it's a video. He's alone on our bed, protected by a wall of pillows, and he's waving his legs and hands around and looking at the ceiling. In the background, coming from one of our two computers, I think, Raffi is singing "Apples and Bananas." Our son is laughing, I think, or just exercising his vocal cords. The video goes on for thirty-three seconds, and then he starts to cry and the video stops. It picks up again an hour later, Raffi still in the background, still with "Apples and Bananas," but now he's in his stroller gripping a tiny rattle. In the next photo he's again in the stroller, with a blanket, belted in, and sleeping while I—I think it's me—push his stroller along the street.

Why didn't we take any pictures? The answer, after more than two years, seems obvious. We were busy, we were too worried, too distressed, to think about photos. We used the phone only to call people or to look up information. To understand what the neurologists, the pediatricians, the nurses were telling us. To try and get a handle on what was happening to us, and what was happening to our son. What were those drugs they were giving him? Why an electroencephalogram? What did it mean, what could it mean, a four-month-old baby having a seizure? The phone was a device for protection, not memories.

Now and then a doctor would come in and ask my wife to recount for the thousandth time, in as much detail as possible, what had happened at the precise moment of the seizure. The baby was suddenly, convulsively crying, not like his normal crying, he lost consciousness in the car, he stopped responding to her, then his head jerked a few times, then nothing. And then they'd examine him, check his pupils, confirm that he responded to stimuli, that he kicked when he should kick, that his arms rose like they were supposed to. We tried to distract him, make him laugh. When the doctors left, we'd look up the words they'd used on our phone.

3.

I stop my writing to confirm that there really are four days of undoc-
umented memories in January 2020. Since that time, I've had to
change my phone twice, so the photographs are still there, except
for the simple fact that they aren't actually *there*, but someplace else,
in the cloud. The hole in our family memory is stored in an accessi-
ble place in the Earth's atmosphere. And that's where it will stay, as
long as I keep paying my ninety-nine-cent monthly fee. If I stopped
paying, it would dissolve. This absence of memory, preserved between
the last photo on January 22 and the first video on January 26, would
cease to be. The gap wouldn't be documented anymore, either. And
maybe we'd gain some peace.

The first documented memory on my phone, which I assume
coincides with our cloud subscription, is from January 8, two weeks
before the twenty-second. It's my first American day, the day we
moved from Rome to Houston. The photograph includes our son,
of course. His stroller sits in front of our first American house. The
stroller takes up a very small portion of the photo, to get the whole
house inside the frame. It's a big house: two stories. What I always
imagined the American dream might look like.

There are maybe a dozen photos with a stroller strangely aban-
doned by the two steps that lead to the front door, and our son's face,
not quite visible. Was he sleeping? Probably, or we wouldn't have
been able to leave him there, ten meters away from us, without spark-
ing a teary short circuit. Was he crying? I stop writing a moment,
pick up my phone, and expand the photo with my fingers. He's not
crying: his eyes are open, pacifier in his mouth.

I sent this picture to my closest friends almost immediately after
I took it. Here you go—my American dream. The house is large,
the front yard well-groomed in its way, at least in the way an Italian
would expect. I don't have my friends' answers—those aren't in the

cloud. But I do remember how consistent they all were. Everyone wrote back: It's like being in a movie.

Except the house isn't ours—it's an Airbnb we rented our first month so we could take our time looking for a place. And we lived in only one section of that house. A third of it, I think, on the first floor. A foyer, a walk-through bedroom, and a kitchen with a stove top, and a washer and dryer.

There's another photo of the bedroom that's saved on my phone and in the cloud. It's of me changing my son's diaper on the bed. Actually, his diaper's already been changed. I'm leaning over him, and he's laughing, mouth open. The photo was taken from above; I'm kneeling at the foot of the bed. The next one, still from January 8, is a night shot of my first American walk. It shows a sign, BAMBOLINO'S. PIZZA BY THE SLICE, with an Italian flag painted on it.

Generally speaking, our son's the model in every photo. On January 9, he's sleeping in his stroller in the kitchen. Behind him: the furniture in this furnished apartment we've rented, including a small bookshelf with fantasy novels, *The Little Prince*, books about the Texas landscape and local restaurants, and a photo book about Houston's struggle with Hurricane Ike, in 2008, with pictures of flooded streets and submerged cars and Texans hard at work getting things back to normal. What's not in this photo I took: the number of times I circled the apartment pushing him in his stroller singing "Passerotto non andare via": "Don't Go, Sparrow." Don't go, sparrow, in your eyes the sun's already dying. Not exactly a children's song, but it works: around the tenth or eleventh rendition, our son's asleep.

Still January 9, I assume after he's woken up, and I'm flying him around the house. Thirteen photos, many out of focus. In some, he's looking at the ceiling just above his head; in others, he's laughing. A mother's photos of a happy father. The photos on January 10 are almost entirely of pickup trucks, plus one old, parked Buick. Then there's me getting our son to nap, rocking him in my arms. Then he's in his froggy chair, beaming at us, laughing, his sleep short-lived. Then Mommy's holding him after his bath, and he's grinning while wrapped in a towel.

I expand the picture with my fingers until there's only my son's face. I cut out everything else—my wife, the furnished apartment, America. Now, two years later, I study his face for a premonition of what would come. With my fingers, I expand the face of a happy child, break it down into its parts: a nose, mouth, and eyes. I look for hints of a seizure in that crease between his lips. In some shots from January 10, the left side of his mouth droops a little. Should we have worried? In retrospect, that smile is more of a grimace—a symptom, then. We thought this only when we studied the pictures after. But that same picture, when we took it—that face—made us laugh for days.

January 11, nearly all of them selfies in a Honda dealership. I'm holding him, while my wife handles the paperwork for our new car. Behind us, display models of various sizes and colors. What's not in the photo: all the dealerships we went to that day. We'd test-driven a number of SUVs, thinking we'd buy one used. An SUV seemed like the proper defense weapon to avoid being overpowered by all the pickups on the highway. But we found them scary to drive—we weren't ready for that leap in size. The selfies in the Honda dealership are the evidence of our failure: our purchase of a compact car.

January 12, our son in his froggy again (nine pictures) or in his stroller in front of our new Honda. The thirteenth, his stroller is in front of the Menil Collection. Again, to get in the entire building designed by Renzo Piano, we zoomed out, so you can barely see the stroller. Still January 13, the photo of my Social Security number: I'm now fitted for the American bureaucratic machine.

January 15, I took fifteen pictures. All at the pediatrician's office. A checkup, our son on his back on the small exam table. The pediatrician hasn't come in yet, and the nurse hasn't given him his vaccination. He's happy; the photos are mainly to document the view out the window. Skyscrapers, downtown Houston. America. What the pediatrician had to say wasn't documented, everything's good, he's a healthy, happy baby. Still the fifteenth, a photo of Bellaire High School. The entryway, the American flag, the Texas flag, both drooping. The school's closed. A shooting the day before. One student killed another, an older kid. An accident, they say, he was showing off his handgun. A marquee by the front doors announces performances January 23–25 (6:30 p.m.) of *Urinetown*.

The following days, the photos are like all the others: cars, baby, skyscrapers, houses. January 18, our son in his stroller holding a piece of paper that says, "Happy birthday, Zio Adelelmo." His eyes peek up over the paper, staring into the lens. In the fourth photo, he's laughing. I enlarge the image, focus on the mouth—but no, his smile is just a baby's smile. On the twentieth, I'm holding my son over my head, the Gulf of Mexico behind me. We're in Galveston. My wife nurses him on a bench.

January 22, our son reads a cloth-bound book in his stroller.

4.

And of those four days, there's not one trace in the journal I kept for a few weeks when we first arrived in Houston. The truth is, I stopped writing in this journal, after very quickly filling almost forty pages with notes. Those pages say no more than my saved photos do. The American dream, houses with front lawns, pickup trucks, and us, the only people in Texas out walking around; they call us the Europeans. When they hear me speak or sing in Italian while I push my son's stroller, they say, "Ciao, bambino." That sort of thing. There's a note on March 9: "I still can't write about what happened." Rather than stopping, it's more like the journal starts to sink; then it goes under.

## 5.

Our son is fine. While I write this, he's at day care. I stopped writing to get him dressed and into the car. He's going through a difficult time right now: he has trouble falling asleep at night, wants us close by until he drifts off. If we step out of the room—what we always did until ten days ago, no problem—he'll burst into desperate wailing. He's also learning how to use the potty. He struggles, sometimes triumphs, sometimes languishes if he fails. We search for advice, on Google and in T. Berry Brazelton's *Touchpoints: Birth to Three*. Everything appears normal, what happens at two. It will pass, this phase will also pass. Another will take its place. We call our Italian pediatrician for advice. He says, "Stay calm. He's going to be fine. He's talking a lot." There's apparently an American method and an Italian method for bed and going potty. I tell my wife, "He's half-Italian and half-American. When he has to pee, let's say he's Italian."

But our son is fine. When I pick him up at day care at four o'clock, they always tell me, "He had a great day." He comes home full of energy, running, jumping. He always wants us around, but it's hard for him if we're both there at the same time. When we're both playing with him, he's convinced, paradoxically, that the attention he gets is halved instead of doubled. He'll send us away. "Mommy, go in the kitchen," he says if he's playing with me. I point out that I'm the one who cooks. To me he'll say, "Go take a shower." Google tells us everything's fine, everything's normal. Stay calm; we're calm. Work on establishing autonomy, if you can.

And our son's seizure—not one trace of it has ever been found in his brain tissue. Not in the hospital, not later. Our entire time at the hospital, they studied his brain for temporary or permanent damage. We played with him, his head covered in electrodes searching for what had happened. From his head, these electrodes, connected to a machine and monitor, produced numbers and graphics that we had no idea how to interpret. Someone would come in once in a while, check on things, leave again. And we kept playing, my wife singing, "I've Been Working on the Railroad," her forehead against our son's forehead. During that time, I learned to cry on the inside while outside I'd laugh to make him laugh, and he'd laugh beneath the electrodes.

And yet not one trace of that seizure remains. Not even the MRI—searching for a "possible mass," so to speak—showed anything. He entered that machine compliantly asleep, after I'd sung to him over and over, "Passerotto non andare via," "Don't Go, Sparrow," crying inside, singing coming from my mouth, in one breath, until his breathing grew heavy and they carried him away on the stretcher, my wife going with him, while I was directed to a waiting room.

There was a football game playing on a huge flat-screen TV. They were running around, beating the living shit out of each other. I don't remember who was playing. But they were running around, beating the living shit out of each other. America. I didn't take any photos in there either. And I thought about nothing tied to my son. I'd have collapsed. But I did think about everything else I'd considered to be the most painful for me—my dysfunctional family, my past fears, my father's violence—and all of it suddenly meant very little. I'd devoted at least four novels and years of therapy to escaping what I'd always considered to be unbearably painful. And now, in the presence of what we were going through in that hospital, it was nothing but gossip.

6.

Our son is fine; we don't know what happened. To this day, the only remaining trace of his seizure is my wife's account. The baby was suddenly, convulsively crying, not like his normal crying, he lost consciousness in the car, he stopped responding to her, then his head jerked a few times, then nothing. The doctors told us it's only this description that permits them to say this was a seizure. That maybe it would be useful to subject him to another electroencephalogram, a longer one, to test his brain activity over the course of twenty-four hours. A young neurologist examined our son a couple of weeks later and told us that, truthfully, he didn't think another EEG was warranted.

The story ends with a final visit to this young neurologist, a month after our son was hospitalized. Our son recognizes him, smiles, plays. The doctor checks that his reflexes are functioning. He examines our son quietly. His hands are gentle, his long fingers pressing down on our baby's limbs. He asks if we've noticed anything abnormal in his behavior, his expressions. We show him the photos with the left part of his mouth pulled down. The ones before he was hospitalized, and some after. The doctor looks at the pictures. Then he tickles our son, who laughs. The doctor says, "He's probably just trying out different faces." At the end of the exam, he asks us to get him dressed and then he tells us there's not much more to say. There's nothing, really, that can document what happened. But what we described, he insists, was definitely a seizure.

"And so?" we ask.

"And so babies are mysterious. That's all I can tell you."

And then there's the three of us driving home, taking a different route to avoid the House of Pies, even if the GPS lady is directing me, in Italian, to go that way. Then there's the January 26 video, with my son on the bed waving his legs and arms around while Raffi sings "Apples and Bananas." No more photos of pickup trucks. And we've never gone back to the House of Pies.

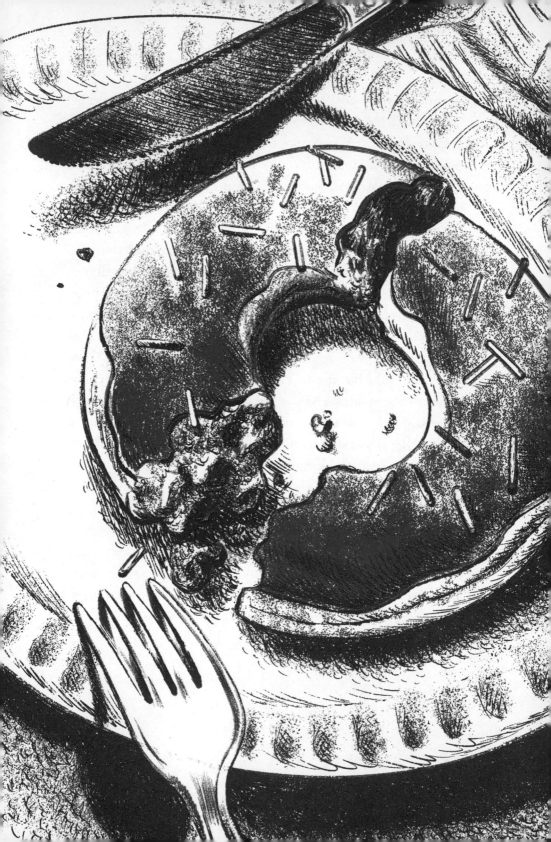

# I EAT IT ALL
# THE TIME

*by* JAMES YEH

ONE DAY AT THE café, Charles is absorbed by a small drama going
on at the table next to him. A father around his age sits frustrated
with his little girl and a woman, who, based on her sparkly ring and
secondary role, he assumes must be the stepmother. The dad ricochets
between hectoring and hugging the little girl; at one point, he gives
her a stern talking-to. In response, she crosses her arms, turning her
back to the adults in a precocious, diva-ish way, and this amuses the
father—he pulls her close.

Watching all this play out, Charles feels not unlike the little girl:
wounded and wound-up, wounded and wound-up. He catches her,
while the father is away, burying her face in her hands. Then rapidly
wiping her eyes before his return.

Asks the wife: Is the sauce a chipotle sauce?

It's a ginger sauce, answers the man. I eat it all the time.

Suddenly his brow furrows violently.

So you're going to just sit there and not eat? He yanks the little
girl's seat so she is right up next to him.

This is the worst thing I've ever seen, he goes on. You're embarrassing us in the restaurant.

Here's the thing: Charles can't stand to hear it, but it's also none of his business. He's not the hero of this story, just some guy at the table beside them, listening in. So what that he, too, has a kid, a son who lives with the mother, which is why Charles now cares about children? This little girl and her dad, and to a lesser extent the stepmom—now speaking quiet Spanish to the little girl—they're the ones who this is really about. If the stepmom is secondary, Charles is tertiary, more or less last. The little girl looks over at him, this curious stranger next to them, and the friendly stranger squeezes a smile. Rueful but, he hopes, reassuring.

When the father goes for forks, his daughter chases after him, anxious. When they get back, she feeds him a fry. She holds out her hand, patiently, painterly, as though finishing her masterpiece.

He takes it.

ANDREA BAJANI is one of the most respected novelists and poets in contemporary Italian literature. He is the author of four novels and three collections of poems. His novel *If You Kept a Record of Sins*, translated by Elizabeth Harris and published in the US by Archipelago Books, won the Mondello Prize, the Brancati Prize, the Recanati Prize, and the Lo Straniero Prize. His works have been translated into many languages and have been published by Gallimard, Anagrama, MacLehose Press, Fraktura, Atheneum, DTV, and Humanitas. He is currently the writer in residence at Rice University in Houston.

Born and raised in Florida, LAURA VAN DEN BERG is the author of five works of fiction, including *The Third Hotel* (Farrar, Straus and Giroux, 2018), which was a finalist for the New York Public Library Young Lions Fiction Award, and *I Hold a Wolf by the Ears* (Farrar, Straus and Giroux, 2020). She is the recent recipient of a Guggenheim Fellowship, a Strauss Livings Award from the American Academy of Arts and Letters, and a literature fellowship from the National Endowment for the Arts.

WILLIAM BREWER is the author of *The Red Arrow*, published by Knopf.

ANNA FITZPATRICK is an occasionally employed Toronto-based writer. She is the author of the children's book *Margot and the Moon Landing* and the novel *Good Girl*.

HALLIE GAYLE is a writer from Texas. Throughout her adult life, she has lived in Southern California, South Africa, and Vietnam. She earned a degree in English from Whittier College and is currently an MFA candidate in fiction at the University of California, Irvine.

ELIZABETH HARRIS's recent translations from the Italian include works by Andrea Bajani, Francesco Pacifico, Claudia Durastanti, and Antonio Tabucchi, for Archipelago Books; Riverhead Books; Fitzcarraldo Editions; Text; and Farrar, Straus and Giroux. Her grants and prizes include an National Endowment for the Arts translation fellowship, a

PEN America translation grant, the Italian Prose in Translation Award, and the National Translation Award.

LISA KO is the author of *The Leavers*, which was a National Book Award for Fiction finalist and won the PEN/Bellwether Prize for Socially Engaged Fiction. Her short fiction has appeared in *Best American Short Stories* and her essays and nonfiction in the *New York Times*, the *Believer*, and elsewhere. Her second novel is forthcoming from Riverhead Books.

CATHERINE LACEY is the author of four books, most recently the novel *Pew*. She lives in New York and Mexico.

CARMEN MARIA MACHADO is the author of the best-selling memoir *In the Dream House* and the award-winning short-story collection *Her Body and Other Parties*. She has been a finalist for the National Book Award and the winner of the Bard Fiction Prize, the Lambda Literary Award for Lesbian Fiction, and the National Book Critics Circle's John Leonard Prize, among other prizes. Her essays, fiction, and criticism have appeared in the *New Yorker*, the *New York Times*, *Granta*, *Vogue*, the *Believer*, and *Guernica*, on *This American Life*, and elsewhere. She holds an MFA from the Iowa Writers' Workshop and has been awarded fellowships and residencies from the Guggenheim Foundation, Yaddo, Hedgebrook, and the Millay Colony for the Arts.

ANDREW MARTIN is the author of the novel *Early Work* and the story collection *Cool for America*. He is at work on a new novel.

MEGAN MCDOWELL has translated many of the most important Latin American writers working today. Her translations have won the English PEN award and the Premio Valle Inclán, and have been nominated four times for the International Booker Prize and once for the Kirkus Prize. In 2020 she won a Literature Award from the American Academy of Arts and Letters. Her short-story translations have been featured in the *New Yorker*, *Harper's Magazine*, the *Paris Review*, *Tin House*, and *Granta*, among other publications. She lives in Santiago, Chile.

SAM RILEY is a TV writer living in Los Angeles.

Using sharp shots of psychological suspense and black humor, SANTIAGO RONCAGLIOLO writes about fear and evil, both in Latin American history and in daily life. In English, he has published the novel *Red April* (which won the Alfaguara Prize and the Independent Foreign Fiction Prize) and the short-story collection *Hi, This Is Conchita*, both translated by Edith Grossman. Roncagliolo is also author of the non-fiction work *Memorias de una dama*, considered "the last censored book of Latin America." *Granta* magazine named him one of its Best Young Spanish Novelists, and the *Guardian* called *Red April* one the best novels about Peru ever translated into English. He lives in Barcelona, where he works as novelist and screenwriter.

DAVE SCHILLING is a humorist and contributing writer for the *Los Angeles Times' Image* magazine. His work has also appeared in the *New Yorker*, the *Guardian*, *New York* magazine, and *GQ*. He lives in Los Angeles with his girlfriend, son, and two underground parking spots.

SRESHTHA SEN is a poet from Delhi, and one of the founding editors of the *Shoreline Review*, an online journal for and by South Asian poets. They studied English literature at Delhi University and completed their MFA at Sarah Lawrence College, in New York. Their work can be found or is forthcoming in *Apogee*, *BOAAT*, *Hyperallergic*, *Hyphen*, the *Margins*, and the *Rumpus*, on Bitch Media, and elsewhere. They were the 2017–18 Readings & Workshops fellow at *Poets & Writers* and currently teach in Las Vegas, where they're completing a PhD in poetry.

JOEL STREICKER's stories have been published in a number of journals, including *Great Lakes Review*, *Gravel*, *Burningword*, and *New Flash Fiction Review*. He won *Blood Orange Review*'s inaugural fiction contest in 2020, and his winning story in *Cutthroat*'s Rick DeMarinis Short Story Contest will appear in the spring of 2022. He has published poetry in both English and Spanish, including the collection *El amor en los tiempos de Belisario* (Bogotá: Común Presencia). His translations of Latin American writers, including Samanta Schweblin, Mariana Enríquez, and Pilar Quintana, have appeared in *A Public Space* and other journals, and his essays have appeared in the *Forward* and *Shofar*, among other publications.

STEPHANIE ULLMANN teaches and writes in Baltimore. She has an MFA from Johns Hopkins. Her story in this issue is based on research funded by a 2010 Spencer T. and Ann W. Olin Fellowship for Women in Graduate Study from Wesleyan University.

JAMES YEH is a writer, editor, and journalist. His nonfiction appears in the *New York Times*, the *Guardian*, and the *Believer*, and his fiction appears in the *Drift*, *Tin House*, and *NOON*. A former editor at the *Believer* and *VICE*, he teaches writing at Columbia University and will be the visiting editor of Issue 69 of this magazine. He lives in Brooklyn, New York.

RACHEL YODER is the author of *Nightbitch*, longlisted for the PEN/ Hemingway Award for Debut Novel and the VCU Cabell First Novelist Award. She is also a founding editor of *draft: the journal of process*. She grew up on a Mennonite commune in the Appalachian foothills of eastern Ohio and now lives in Iowa City.

ALEJANDRO ZAMBRA is the author of six works of fiction, including *Multiple Choice*, *My Documents*, and *Chilean Poet*. The recipient of numerous literary prizes and a New York Public Library Cullman Center fellowship, he has published stories in the *New Yorker*, the *New York Times Magazine*, the *Paris Review*, *Granta*, and *Harper's Magazine*, among other publications. He lives in Mexico City.

*"Solar power, wind power, the power of the imagination—it's going to take lots of energy for us to grapple with the challenge we're facing, and some of it is on vivid display in these pages."*
—Bill McKibben

## McSWEENEY'S 58: 2040 A.D.

*McSweeney's 58: 2040 A.D.* is wholly focused on climate change, with speculative fiction from ten contributors, made in collaboration with the Natural Resources Defense Council. Using fiction—informed here and there by realism and climate science—this issue explores the tangible, day-to-day implications of these cataclysmic scientific projections. Featuring Tommy Orange, Elif Shafak, Luis Alberto Urrea, Asja Bakić, Rachel Heng, and others.

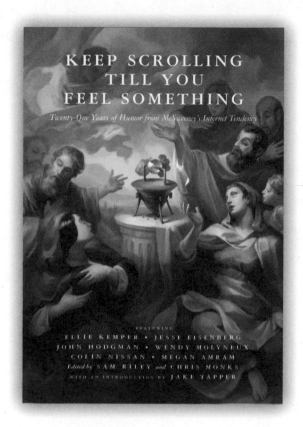

# ALSO AVAILABLE
# FROM McSWEENEY'S

## NONFICTION

## VOICE OF WITNESS

## HUMOR

# ALL THIS AND MORE AT

STORE.MCSWEENEYS.NET

Founded in 1998, McSweeney's is an independent publisher based in San Francisco. McSweeney's exists to champion ambitious and inspired new writing, and to challenge conventional expectations about where it's found, how it looks, and who participates. We're here to discover things we love, help them find their most resplendent form, and place them into the hands of curious, engaged readers.

THERE ARE SEVERAL WAYS TO SUPPORT MCSWEENEY'S:

Support Us on Patreon
visit *www.patreon.com/mcsweeneysinternettendency*

Subscribe & Shop
visit *store.mcsweeneys.net*

Volunteer & Intern
email *eric@mcsweeneys.net*

Sponsor Books & *Quarterlies*
email *amanda@mcsweeneys.net*

To learn more, please visit *www.mcsweeneys.net/donate*
or contact Executive Director Amanda Uhle at
*amanda@mcsweeneys.net* or 415.642.5609.

McSweeney's Literary Arts Fund is a nonprofit
organization as described by IRS 501(c)(3).
Your support is invaluable to us.